Lives in Two Languages

An Exploration of Identity and Culture

Linda Watkins-Goffman

Ann Arbor

THE UNIVERSITY OF MICHIGAN PRESS

Lives in Two Languages

Contents

Why This Book

Writing occurs as a reaction to a lived life experience. The idea for this book came while I was teaching a course for teachers of bilingual children on the topic of the psychological and sociological processes of the bilingual experience. The books by Rodriguez (*Hunger of Memory*), Hoffman (*Lost in Translation*), Tan (*The Joy Luck Club*), and Lee (*Native Speaker*) were required reading in the course. As we read these books in class, the students and I were continually amazed by the sensitivity to issues of identity and culture that these authors revealed. Topics such as public and private identity, the splitting and triangulating of identity, and other strategies that immigrant students use came out of the discussions and my own research.

Later, I decided to add texts by Alvarez, Hurston, and others to focus on other topics such as gender, immigration, race, and class because while these are discussed to some extent, they were not as completely explored in the other books assigned in the course. I field tested this new material and the original writers in my teacher-training classes, and my students were amazed and enthusiastic about how much they learned from all the writers. They felt the words in these excerpts gave them insight into the nature of the experience of their students, who were coping with identity in two cultures. In fact, many teacher trainees felt the topic of identity was truly compelling and integral to the development of voice in the students, as well as the integrity and authenticity in the teacher's own sense of identity. As a result of becoming completely immersed in the material, I became more aware of my own identity and began researching and writing fiction based on a renewed sense of self. I hope you have a similar experience.

Journal Writing

Throughout this book, you will be given questions for journal writing. This means that you can write your reaction, responses, and comments that relate to the questions in a spontaneous way. You need not be worried about editing for grammar, punctuation, and spelling at this initial stage. This writing could also be used as a springboard for discussion. In addition, your journal writings could develop into a draft for a finished, edited paper at your professor's discretion.

You will also see, interspersed throughout the book, drafts that are edited compilations of the journal writings of my students over the years. You may use these as models for your own journal and as examples of the multiple perspectives of other students. Though this book was originally intended for educators and teachers of immigrant and English as a Second Language students, it would be appropriate for anyone who is interested in issues about culture and identity; for example, anyone who is studying for a career in the social sciences would benefit as well.

I would have preferred, had time and space permitted, to include entire books instead of excerpts. Instead, I was forced to use excerpts that illuminated the issues of identity I felt were most important to educators. I strongly recommend that students—and teachers—read each of the books excerpted in this text in its entirety, as my students and I originally did. There is much to be learned from these writers and others who live or have lived *Lives in Two Languages.*

Acknowledgments

Without the help of many people, it would have been impossible to write this book. I am grateful to Kelly Sippell, acquisitions editor at the University of Michigan Press, who was enthusiastic about this project from the start. I thank Liz Suhay and Nichole Argyres, who helped with permissions.

I would like to acknowledge the many students who have graciously given feedback on the drafts as the book evolved and whose writing appears throughout this text as journal entry composites. I also thank my husband, Richard Goffman, whose encouragement and editing skills helped bring my ideas into reality.

Thanks also to Professor Cynthia Jones of Hostos Community College (CUNY) for all of her advice on Chapter 7.

I also wish to acknowledge the writers whose excerpted texts appear in this book. Their ideas have taught me much; the way I think about culture and identity has changed forever.

Grateful acknowledgment is made to the following for permission to reprint previously published material.

Susan Bergholz Literary Services for "I Want to Be Miss America," from *Something to Declare.* Copyright © 1998 by Julia Alvarez. Published by Algonquin Books of Chapel Hill, 1998. Reprinted by permission of Susan Bergholz Literary Services, New York, and Luitingh Sihthoff Publishers. All rights reserved.

David R. Godine, Publisher, for excerpt from *Hunger of Memory* by Richard Rodriguez. Reprinted by permission of David R. Godine, Publisher, Inc. Copyright © 1982 by Richard Rodriguez.

HarperCollins Publishers for Chapter 12 "My People! My People!" from *Dust Tracks on a Road* by Zora Neale Hurston. Copyright 1942 by Zora Neale Hurston. Copyright renewed 1970 by John C. Hurston. Reprinted by permission of HarperCollins Publishers, Inc.

The New Press for excerpt of "From the Far Side" by Mark Mathabane. Copyright © 1992 *Race: How Blacks and Whites Feel about the American Obsession* by Studs Terkel. Reprinted by permission of The New Press.

Newsweek magazine for permission to reprint "Who Is a Whiz Kid?" by Ted Gup.

Penguin Putnam Inc. and the Random House Archive and Library for excerpt from *Lost in Translation* by Eva Hoffman. Copyright © 1989 by Eva Hoffman. Used by permission of Dutton, a division of Penguin Putnam Inc.

Penguin Putnam Inc. for excerpt from *Native Speaker* by Chang-rae Lee. Copyright © 1995 by Chang-rae Lee. Used by permission of Putnam Berkley, a division of Penguin Putnam Inc., and by permission of International Creative Management, Inc.

Putnam Publishing Group and Abner Stein for excerpt from *The Joy Luck Club* by Amy Tan. Reprinted by permission of G. P. Putnam's Sons, a division of Penguin Putnam Inc. from *The Joy Luck Club* by Amy Tan. Copyright © 1989 by Amy Tan.

May Stawsky for permission to print her essay.

Every effort has been made to trace the ownership of all copyrighted material in this book and to obtain permission for its use.

Chapter 1
An Introduction to Identity and Culture

Identity is a complex ongoing mental process influenced by one's experiences. One's history and experiences are key to the sense of self. Our identity or who we feel we are is important because it is at the core of all our thoughts and feelings and it influences how we express them. Someone who has emigrated,* for example, probaby has a more complex sense of identity than does someone who has lived in the same place since birth. As a result, those individuals who work with students who are immigrants, such as English as a second language (ESL) and bilingual education (BE) teachers, need to better understand the psychological process that accompanies the immigrant experience in order to be able to connect with their students. Teachers need to recognize that as the students struggle to learn the language and adapt to a new culture, they are also searching for an identity in a new cultural context and often in a very short amount of time.

Psychosocial Phenomenon

Salman Akhtar, a psychiatrist who describes himself as "an immigrant analyst . . . with his own hybrid identity" (1996, 1075), has explored the psychosocial phenomenon in his work as a therapist. According to Akhtar, immigration from one country to another is a complex psychosocial process with lasting effects on a person's identity. Although he was focusing on adults in his paper, his findings can also apply to children who are immigrants. In fact, regardless of age, immigrant students can go through a variety of psychological and linguistic processes and responses in order to cope with the demands of a new culture. This book will explore these processes in order to help the professionals who work with immigrants bet-

*To emigrate is to leave one country and settle in another. In contrast, to immigrate is to come to a country where one is not native to take up permanent residence.

ter understand them and help them adjust to the new culture, including the expectations of that culture.

The process of acculturation,* or adjusting one's native culture to a new one, is further complicated by the sociocultural context of the individual, which includes considering such variables as size of the native language group to which the immigrant belongs in this country and whether that group is seen as subordinate politically, culturally, technically, or economically (Schumann 1978). In fact, an immigrant group might be held in esteem in one area of the country where there are few representatives of that culture. There, individuals in that group might be seen as exotic and "interesting"; in contrast, where the same culture's population is large and economically deprived, they may be seen as subordinate socially to the more affluent cultural group.

The acculturation process and the forming of a new identity belong not *[Acc not only for moving from 1 country to another but from 1 part to another of the same country]* only to those who emigrate to this country from another; they can also affect those who move from one part of this country to another. For example, those who emigrate to the North from the southern United States, which has its own distinct subculture, can experience a difficult acculturation process (Silber 1993, 5).

Question for Writing and Discussion

Take 15 minutes and write what you know about the cultural context of someone you know. If you were not born in the United States, you may use yourself. Tell what you guess to be the size of the individual's language population. Write your opinion about the American perception of that group, politically, culturally, or economically. Are Americans welcoming to the specified immigrant group, and how does the perception vary from region to region?

Performance in the Classroom and Overcompensation

Psychosocial processes that the immigrant experiences can often be complicated by overcompensatory behaviors that resemble the ambivalence of

---

*Acculturation is the process of adapting the cultural traits or social patterns of another group, but retaining aspects of the native culture as well. Assimilation means the absorption of one's native cultural traits into the new culture.

[handwritten margin note: Comparison]

an adolescent trying to flee from the parent's apron strings (Akhtar 1995, 1051). Like all human development, the process proceeds along a continuum, is recursive, and is unique to the individual and the respective culture. For teachers, performance in the classroom, particularly when driven by motivation, is controlled by the emotional and psychological state of the individual student. Therefore, teachers need to learn to gain another perspective so that they can better understand the inner lives of their students. Once this perspective is gained, a connection is formed, and through this bond, communication is improved, which can result in increased efficiency in the classroom and better academic performance.

Learning Perspective from Immigrant Writers: Introducing Richard Rodriguez

Often, the necessary perspective is gained through reading about the immigrant experience and viewing it depicted on the movie screen. Recently there have been a number of noteworthy books, both autobiographical and fictional, about immigrants acculturating here in the United States. Often complicated psychological processes, such as the identification of public and private selves, have been the topic of talented bilingual writers. In *Lives in Two Languages*, we will be discussing writers such as Richard Rodriguez, Eva Hoffman, Chang-rae Lee, and Amy Tan. This section will preview the writers that will be discussed in this book.

[handwritten margin note: In their work = central themes]

Richard Rodriguez, a first-generation Mexican American growing up in the 1950s in California, experienced the acculturation process as a child once the nuns in the Catholic school he attended asked that his parents use only English when they spoke at home. As a result, Rodriguez lost Spanish, which for him was the language of his home, the language of intimacy. In his book that recounts the story of his acculturation to American culture, *Hunger of Memory*, Rodriguez says,

[handwritten margin note: Theme]

> Most of the people who called me a *pocho* could have spoken English to me. But they would not. They seemed to think that Spanish was the only language we could use, that Spanish alone permitted our close association. (Such persons are vulnerable always to the ghetto merchant and the politician who have learned the value of speaking their clients' family language to gain immediate trust.) For my part, I felt that I had somehow committed a sin of betrayal by learning English. But betrayal against whom? Not against visitors to the house exactly. No, I felt that I had betrayed my immediate family. I *knew* that my par-

[handwritten margin note: Fighting he + his self]

ents had encouraged me to learn English. I *knew* that I had turned to English only with angry reluctance. But once I spoke English with ease, I came to *feel* guilty. (This guilt defied logic.) I felt that I had shattered the intimate bond that had once held the family close. This original sin against my family told whenever anyone addressed me in Spanish and I responded, confounded. (1983, 30)

According to sociologist Erving Goffman (1959), the public identity of an individual is different from the personality that is shown to intimates. For immigrants, this distinction is more intense, in part because of the effort to adjust the individual's native identity and language to those of the host culture. In *Hunger of Memory,* Rodriguez eloquently describes the price he paid for learning the public language (English) at the expense of the private (Spanish). Yet his reaction is not that different from what many immigrant children experience when they feel conflicted about the rejection or the belittling of their own native language, the language they use with those who are close to them. Many immigrants attempt to integrate their public and private identities as a key to successful acculturation; that is, they have to learn to take pride in both public and private languages, just as they need to feel comfortable with both identities. For example, a child should feel comfortable using Spanish when speaking to his or her mother, as an intimate language, and English when speaking in the classroom, as a public language. The child thus claims identity as a private speaker of Spanish and a public speaker of English. However, this can mean months and years of ambiguity, until the child feels comfortable with both identities and the social contexts in which each belongs.

In order to be able to tolerate this ambiguity, students often adopt a number of coping devices, such as what Gee (1992) calls "mushfaking," which means making do with the resources at hand. In other words, not knowing the culture from the inside, they might try to imitate the members of that culture in order to accommodate. This may often involve learning nonverbal signals, that is, signals that communicate without words—for example, body language or gestures such as a hand held up for "hello." Professor Nine-Curt of the Universidad de Puerto Rico at Rio Piedras (1994) says that a member of the dominant culture needs to see something of himself or herself reflected in an individual from an immigrant group, in order for the former to accept the latter. This often means that immigrant students have to become almost like anthropologists, observing nonverbal behavior in the host culture and copying it. For example, laughing in one culture may mean something totally different in another. Nine-Curt says that Puerto Rican college students smile when they don't understand something someone says in class. Not being familiar with nonverbal signals in Puerto Rican culture, someone from an Anglo culture might misinterpret a smile of confusion as one of contentment (Nine-Curt 1994).

Questions for Writing and Discussion

1. Write about the languages you hear in your schools or neighborhoods. Which private languages have you identified? Which public ones?
2. In groups, brainstorm about nonverbal signals (such as hand and head movements, facial expressions, physical closeness between individuals) and how they vary in different cultures. Can your group come up with confusing and ambiguous situations that can result from misunderstanding nonverbal communication?

Introducing Eva Hoffman

Another way of coping with emotional ambiguity and the discomfort of suddenly finding oneself in a new culture is to try to detach oneself from one's surroundings. Feeling all of one's feelings with the normal intensity can be too painful for some immigrants. *[handwritten: detachment from surroundings]*

In chapter 3 we will examine excerpts from Eva Hoffman's autobiography. Hoffman was a successful immigrant who emigrated from Poland in the 1950s to a Jewish ghetto in Vancouver, Canada, and later became an English literary scholar and author. She described her acculturation experiences in her book *Lost in Translation* (1989). On the topic of feeling detached from the self she knew in Poland, Hoffman wrote:

> For a long time, confronting the dangers both of self-division and of deprivation, I cultivate a rigorous renunciation. I suppose it serves me well. Like some visiting Indian swami, I learn to measure myself against no one and to feel at home everywhere. Not envying is the condition of my dignity, and I protect that dignity with my life. In a sense, it *is* my life—the only base I have to stand on. If I sometimes have to go around with a run in my stockings when I am in college, if I can't afford the long trek home during Christmas recess, it doesn't matter. I have my essential humanity, that essential humanity which I learned to believe in as a Jewish girl in Poland, and which I've now salvaged with the

help of withdrawal and indifference. "Sometimes I see you with a steel rod running down the middle of your back," a friend once tells me. He sees more than most. (139)

In order to survive and to eventually reach her goal of integrating the new culture with the old, Hoffman often described herself as an anthropologist. She found that she triangulated experiences, or saw them from three perspectives. Depending on whether she was seeing her world as the Polish Ewa or the American Eva, or some emerging sense of self, she felt an entirely different inner experience.

> Nothing has to be the way it is; people could behave in a different manner; I could look different, flirt differently; I could be having entirely different conversations. Not any specific conversations; the other place in my mind no longer has any particularity. It's just an awareness that there is another place—another point at the base of the triangle, which renders this place relative, which locates me within that relativity itself. (1989, 170)

Questions for Writing and Discussion

1. What are other defensive mechanisms that might be useful to immigrants or to anyone who is becoming accustomed to a new environment and is experiencing ambiguity, confusion, and other negative emotions? Share your answers with the class.
2. Have you ever moved to another city or neighborhood? Can you remember what you felt at the time about leaving home and friends behind? Describe your feelings before, during, and after the move.

Introducing Chang-rae Lee

In chapter 6, we will see the complexity of possible responses that immigrants use in order to accommodate themselves to an alien culture. Chang-rae Lee, in his novel *Native Speaker,* makes his protagonist a spy, someone who vicariously lives other lives as an occupation. Feeling that he is neither Korean nor American, Henry Park, the spy, assumes a safe "middle ground" and creates the detachment that Hoffman achieved through triangulation. The story is a metaphor for the assumed identity or identities that many immigrants feel they have to take on as a means of surviving in the mainstream world. Of his spy Henry Park, Lee writes:

And yet you may know me. I am an amiable man. I can be most personable, if not charming, and whatever I possess in this life is more or less the result of a talent I have for making you feel good about yourself when you are with me. In this sense I am not a seducer. I am hardly seen. I won't speak untruths to you, I won't pass easy compliments or odious offerings of flattery. I make do with on-hand materials, what I can chip out of you, your natural ore. Then I fuel the fire of your most secret vanity. (1995, 7)

Another characteristic seen in many successful immigrants is the tendency to overcompensate. This can be seen, for instance, in students who push themselves to the extreme. For some, this drive is an attempt to find a second chance at success, an attempt to reinvent themselves in a new culture. Amati-Mehler, Argentieri, and Canestri (1993) concluded that

The tendency to overcompensate S.D. else in the new Creature

> A multilingual dimension certainly does allow for an internal enrichment not only at the cognitive level. However, it is also true that the actual mental organization of the multilingual subject lends itself in particular to the enacting of defenses, splittings and repressions. Occasionally a new language represents a life saving anchor which allows for "rebirth," at other times it can be a justification for the mutilation of the internal world of the self. (1993, 108)

how new S.D. can be seen

Eva Hoffman, who well knew the pressure to succeed, was gifted both in music and in language. When it was time to select a profession, she decided to pursue a literary career in her second language.

> I, too, suffer from the classic immigrant misconception, and I can't distinguish between the normal and the strenuous road in life, between moderate and high achievement. Becoming a lawyer seems to me as difficult as becoming a chief justice, a teacher of freshman English is as august a personage in my world as a college president. I don't envision that I can get to any of these exalted positions by an ordinary sequence of steps, but by putting one foot in front of the other. I have to drive myself, to be constantly on the alert. (1989, 158)

Akhtar says that the opposite response can also take place. Instead of focusing aggressively on achievement, the immigrant can regress, much like the child returning to its mother's welcoming arms. Idealization of the native country and culture can occur. For example, many immigrants have a kind of shrine in their home with pictures and objects from their homeland.

> [The immigrant's] most powerful affects are reserved for his recall of the houses, street corners, cafes, hills, and the countryside of his homeland. Like the emotionally deprived child, with but one toy, he clings to their memories.

Ever wistful, the immigrant convinces himself that "if only" he had not left these places, his life would have been wonderful or, more frequently, that when he was there he had no problems. (1995, 1065)

Question for Writing and Discussion

Can you think of any specific instances in which an immigrant has idealized his or her native country? You may use any books, movies, or stories of people you know who have come to this country as immigrants. Be prepared to share your writing with the class.

Introducing Amy Tan

Conflict in the acculturating self can lead to a communications gap within the generations, as discussed in chapter 5. In her novel *The Joy Luck Club*, Amy Tan describes the rebellion of four modern, American-born daughters who confront the older values of their mothers. The mothers are conflicted as well, trying to offer a better life to their offspring but watching as their children inevitably make some of the very mistakes they themselves made when they were young.

> And then it occurs to me. They are frightened. In me, they see their own daughters, just as ignorant, just as unmindful of all the truths and hopes they have brought to America. They see daughters who grow impatient when their mothers talk in Chinese, who think they are stupid when they explain things in fractured English. They see that joy and luck do not mean the same to their daughters, that to these closed American-born minds "joy luck" is not a word, it does not exist. They see daughters who will bear grandchildren born without any connecting hope passed from generation to generation. (1989, 31)

Question for Writing and Discussion

Have you ever witnessed any intergenerational conflict related to culture or language? You may include books you have read or movies that you have seen or examples from personal experience. Make a five-minute presentation that summarizes what you wrote.

Sociocultural Factors

Even though this text focuses on psychological processes, the sociological context is important to mention. As with all human development, the acculturation process is not linear; rather, the individual shifts back and forth as events change in the everyday cultural context. The individual's progress is affected by the social and economic context. Schumann (1978), in his discussion of second language acquisition, discussed many factors that contribute to the progress that an immigrant makes. Among them are the following: the size of the native language group in the host culture; the attitude with which the immigrant is treated in the host culture; the cultural distance between the two cultures; whether or not the individual can return home; the skills with which the individual came and the marketability of those skills; and the age at which the individual came to this country. Akhtar adds to these characteristics inherent personal ones, such as the psychological flexibility and stability of the immigrant and the extent to which an individual has achieved an intrapsychic capacity for separateness prior to immigration (1995).

Schumann, as part of a larger study, the Harvard project (Cazden et al. 1975), conducted a ten-month observation of the untutored acquisition of English of Alberto, a thirty-three-year-old working class Costa Rican. Alberto, whose intelligence tested in the normal range, was not able to progress past a certain point in the study of English. This caused Schumann to look for other variables that could explain his lack of progress. He found that the following sociocultural factors were at play.

1. *Social dominance.* This refers to the extent to which one social group is politically, economically, culturally, or technically superior to another. Alberto, a lower-class immigrant worker, belonged to a group that was socially subordinate to the host group.
2. *Integration pattern.* The Costa Rican immigrant group had relatively high enclosure. Enclosure is the degree to which a group shares the same churches, schools, clubs, recreational facilities, professions, and so on as another group. Low enclosure means many of these domains are shared. The Costa Ricans in Alberto's group tended not to interact with the host group.
3. *Cohesiveness.* This term also refers to the tendency of the immigrant group to remain separate from the host culture. Alberto was in a fairly cohesive immigrant group; the Costa Ricans had little contact with the target language group.

4. *Attitude.* The attitude between Alberto's group (lower-class immigrant workers) and the host group (middle-class Americans) was at best neutral and at worst hostile.
5. *Intended length of residence.* The plan for Alberto was to stay a short time for job purposes and then return to his native country.
6. *Size.* The group Alberto belonged to was large, therefore not encouraging moving into the host group.
7. *Social distance.* Social distance measures the tendency of an immigrant group to remain apart socially or mix with the host group. The group that Alberto belonged to was socially distant from the host group. The two groups had no social interaction.

Question for Writing and Discussion

What other factors do you think affect acculturation? Make a list and share your ideas with your peers.

The factors identified by Schumann would make acculturation difficult for immigrants like Alberto, such that one coping strategy might be to idealize the native culture and create a nostalgic longing for anything that represents home. Under these negative circumstances, the individual might be reluctant to acculturate and learn the target language. Teachers of ESL students should keep these variables and the coping processes in mind when they teach and should find ways to help students adjust and find a comfortable integration of their two identities into a new one. As Garza-Guerrero says,

> A new identity will reflect the final consolidation into a remodeled ego identity of those selective identifications with the new culture which were harmoniously integrated or fitted in with the past cultural heritage. What actually ensues from the crisis of culture shock, if adequately solved, is a fecund growth of the self. What began as a threat to identity, mourning, and low self-esteem ends in a confirmation of both ego identity and self-esteem. (1974, 425)

More research and primarily case studies are needed to shed light on a complicated cultural phenomenon that influences the learner's progress in the second language classroom. For example, teachers can learn to use ethnographic tools, such as the interview, in order to help students explore emergent identities. Ethnography as a research paradigm in education can help researchers and educators to better understand the issues and to form educational policies and pedagogies that reflect the inner lives of immigrants. The ethnographic interviews of bilingual students in public schools in the Massachusetts area used in Nieto's *Affirming Diversity* (1996) produced interesting parallels to the coping mechanisms of acculturation revealed in the excerpts from books and films, autobiographical in nature, used in this book. The ethnographic interview, if used properly, will cause the story of the individual's psychological experience to emerge. It can be an effective tool for educators and other professionals to learn more about the immigrant's psychological reality.

Identity is an important issue for language learning. Recent research conducted at the City University of New York is testing the hypothesis that the success of second language speakers is mediated by the level of comfort they feel working in that language, as well as how well integrated language use is in positive self-concepts (for example, if a person feels good about herself speaking English). Preliminary feedback suggests that those second language students will do the best whose self-concept does not depend strongly on native language use (Martin 1999).

Questions for Writing and Discussion

1. What do you think it is really like to be an immigrant? Do you think that the factors discussed are present in the acculturation processes of other individuals besides immigrants?
2. Conduct a ten-minute interview with an immigrant. Try to understand the processes that the individual is undergoing in his or her efforts to acculturate. Write a discussion of the leading factors you discovered.

Culture as Enrichment

Though learning to communicate in English is important for immigrants, in order for students to feel at home in the classroom, the curriculum should reflect the ethnic identity of the students in the class as a means of enriching and adding another dimension to the discipline studied. Generally speaking, there should always be a multicultural perspective in the curriculum. For example, teachers can help students verbalize what psychological processes they are undergoing by encouraging introspective journal writing about the acculturation process. In addition, classroom assignments could focus on culture, particularly the students' native cultures, so that the transition might be made more gradual and so that positive feelings about native identity can be supported. For example, research projects, books, and articles could be assigned that are related to the culture and background of students. If a class containing Mexican immigrants is studying ancient cultures in Egypt, a unit on the Maya might be included and comparisons set up between the ancient Maya and Egyptian cultures. In order to design curricula and classes in which students are comfortable, all teachers should be in touch with issues of culture and identity and keep a multicultural, flexible perspective on language identity and culture. Too often, classes full of diverse students are taught by a monolingual, monocultural teacher whose view reflects only their own native identity and culture and fails to connect with students from a minority culture.

Chapter 2
The Public and Private Selves

Introduction

One of the most important issues in the psychological development of the multicultural individual is the emergence of the public and private selves. According to sociologist Erving Goffman (1959), an individual presents an impression to the world much like an actor does to an audience, and in this way a public self is formed. This self will often have its own language, a public language. In addition, there is information about the same person that is known only to intimates, and there is a corresponding private language used only with close associates. For example, many people use their first language with intimates in their homes and use English, the public language, with everyone else. These selves and their corresponding codes can exist in separate domains or overlap (Fishman 1977). For example, one may use the native language only in certain contexts, the new or public language in others, and in situations where the audience is bilingual, switch back and forth or present a message in the public language and whisper to an intimate standing next to the speaker in private language. In this chapter we will explore this issue of public and private self by examining Richard Rodriguez's memoir *Hunger of Memory* and the film *Mi Familia*, directed by Gregory Nava.

In discussing the public self in his book *The Presentation of the Self in Everyday Life* (1959), Goffman says each person creates a public persona and "plays a part" in much the same way that an actor performs in a play:

> When an individual plays a part he implicitly requests his observers to take seriously the impression that is fostered before them. They are asked to believe that the character they see actually possesses the attributes he appears to possess, that the task he performs will have the consequences that are implicitly claimed for it, and that, in general, matters are what they appear to be. In line with this, there is the popular view that the individual offers his performance and puts on his show "for the benefit of other people." (1959, 17)

Goffman goes on to say that to sustain an impression for any audience, certain proprieties must be selected that contribute to the overall picture. These will include dress, timing, manner, and any nonverbal gestures that communicate what the people or actors want to convey; they will also include language or dialect. Goffman says that all communication must be in character so that the impression in the audience's mind is maintained. The choice of language will contribute to the message being given about the role and identity of the actor. Zerubavel corroborates this view in his book *A Fine Line* (1991) when he discusses how people make distinctions at the perceptual level between what is acceptable and what is not, even so far as to decide what is safe and what is not. The public language is perceived as a "common ground" and a safe vehicle for communication, generally speaking.

But what happens when the private language becomes the public language? Richard Rodriguez experienced this; in fact, to a great degree, he lost his native language of Spanish, and English became both his private and public language.

Keeping this in mind, when a bilingual person chooses one or the other of the languages to be the "public language," others will identify the speaker accordingly. The public language will represent the public identity of the speaker. Many who are bilingual will choose one language to be the public language, and it usually is the "official" language of the majority in a given country. The native language will therefore remain the private language, assigned for use with intimates. For example, for most immigrants, the public language and persona are English, and the private language and persona are the native language. Once a person is finished in a public setting or context or acting on a stage, the need for the public language is gone; once a person is within an intimate context where the public forum is not necessary or even welcome, the public language, or language of the world, is dropped. The intimate language, used mostly with people with whom one is in a close relationship, allows the corresponding intimate self, banished while in front of the public, to appear.

However, an individual does not have to be an immigrant to experience a public and private self. One can move, for example, from the country to the city and have the same process occur. One example of a private language or dialect is a strong Southern drawl, which does not always "work" as a public language in Northern cities where it sometimes connotes an uneducated, slow, or eccentric person or other not-so-positive stereotypes.

Questions for Writing and Discussion

In groups, brainstorm, discuss, and write your reactions to the following questions. After you have finished, read aloud to the group what you have written.

1. Are you aware of having a public and private self? In what context do you experience each? Explain, giving specific situations.
2. To whom do you feel you expose your inner feelings and thoughts? What language do you use when you are expressing this intimate side of your personality? Why do you choose it?
3. Describe a situation in which a person could use both his or her public and private languages. Be as specific as you can with regard to setting and language.
4. Discuss your heritage, describing what you know about the public and private languages of your ancestors. Trace these identities to your immediate family and yourself.
5. Explain how culture interacts with the public and private languages.

Student Writing Samples

Here are two sample drafts of answers to questions 1 and 3, respectively.

My grandparents came to the United States from Italy and my parents were born in the United States. I grew up in a family that spoke Italian at family gatherings. My grandparents used Italian words and phrases when they were very happy, very angry or talking about food! The phrases that I recognized and associated with the emotion they portrayed established a bond in our family. To this day, I only know swear words and terms of endearment in Italian because this was a private language. In contrast to my Italian self, my English-speaking self is very different. My English friends tell me that I appear confident, self-assured and calm. I don't think I try to consciously create a public self that is different from the private. Actually, as I am getting older, I find that I am much more comfortable revealing my more emotional private self.

* * *

My everyday routines encompass many different identities, that of teacher, mother, wife, daughter, friend, business owner. Many of my private self identities revolve around code switching between various languages. In Athens, Greece, I grew up in a home where my mother spoke English; my father, who is from the Dominican Republic, spoke Spanish and my friends Greek. My sister and I continue to speak Greek together as I also do with many childhood friends with whom I am still in touch. The music I play at home and in my car is mainly Greek, and it energizes me to confront my working day. My father, mother and I continue to speak Spanish amongst ourselves. The woman who takes care of my children is also Spanish-speaking, as are the people who work in my office. The children in my classroom are mainly Spanish-speaking and throughout the day I use both languages.

Curiously, the only part of my private life which is all in English is the communication with my husband and my children. Both can understand quite a bit of Spanish but refuse to speak it though I continue the battle that my children will learn at least Spanish. I feel more at ease speaking Greek or Spanish and often feel I cannot express myself properly in English, though everyone understands me! I have been living in the USA thirteen years but return frequently overseas to visit friends and family in the Dominican Republic and Greece and also feel very at home!

Compare and contrast the preceding two writers. How are they alike and how are they different with regard to their public and private selves?

Richard Rodriguez's *Hunger of Memory*

In *Hunger of Memory: The Education of Richard Rodriguez* (1983), Richard Rodriguez, a Mexican American lecturer and former college instructor, looks back on his childhood. He was born to Mexican immigrants in Sacramento, California, in the 1950s as Ricardo Rodriguez. He spoke only Spanish until he entered Catholic grade school. In *Hunger of Memory*, the adult Richard remembers the warmth of a household in which Spanish was spoken. However, when the nuns of the Catholic school that he attended asked that his parents use only English at home, Richard derived much from the opportunity to master the public language. Richard's father, who never fully acquired the public language of English, spoke haltingly and with an accent; he embarrassed the teenage Richard. A would-be engineer, Richard's father's academic progress was frustrated by linguistic barriers, and he remained in a series of manual labor positions. Richard's mother was more successful learning English than her husband; she studied typing and office work. She, too, was limited by education, once losing a typing job because of spelling errors. In contrast to her husband, she gained public confidence and identity as a result of having the family convert to English. Richard's brother and sister are shadowy figures in the book and remain in the background only to complete the family circle. Because they were older when English began to be spoken at home, their ties to Spanish remained, and they therefore knew fewer conflicts between public and private identities.

In the following excerpt, Rodriguez remembers the painful process of leaving the language of intimacy (Spanish) and entering a whole new "public world" with English.

I grew up victim to a disabling confusion. As I grew fluent in English, I no longer could speak Spanish with confidence. I continued to understand spoken Spanish. And in high school, I learned how to read and write Spanish. But for many years, I could not pronounce it. A powerful guilt blocked my spoken words; an essential glue was missing whenever I'd try to connect words to form sentences. I would not be able to break a barrier of sound, to speak freely. I would speak, or try to speak Spanish, and I would manage to utter halting, hiccuping sounds that betrayed my unease.

When relatives and Spanish-speaking friends of my parents came to the house, my brother and sisters seemed reticent to use Spanish, but at least they managed to say a few necessary words before being excused. I never managed so gracefully. I was cursed with guilt. Each time I'd hear myself addressed in Spanish, I would be unable to respond with any success. I'd know the words I wanted to say, but I couldn't manage to say them. I would try to speak, but everything I said seemed to me horribly anglicized. My mouth would not form the words right. My jaw would tremble. After a phrase or two, I'd cough up a warm, silvery sound. And stop.

It surprised my listeners to hear me. They'd lower their heads, better to grasp what I was trying to say. They would repeat their questions in gentle, affectionate voices. But by then I would answer in English. "No, no," they would say, "We want you to speak in Spanish." (". . . en español.") But I couldn't do it. *Pocho* then they called me. Sometimes playfully, teasingly, using the tender diminutive—*mi pochito*. Sometimes not so playfully, mockingly, *pocho*. (A Spanish dictionary defines that word as an adjective, meaning "colorless" or "bland." But I hear it as a noun, naming the Mexican-American who, in becoming an American, forgets his native society.) "*Pocho*" the lady in the Mexican food store muttered, shaking her head. I looked up to the counter where red and green peppers were strung like Christmas tree lights and saw the frowning face of the stranger. My mother laughed somewhere behind me. (She said that her children didn't want to practice "our Spanish" after they started going to school.) My mother's smiling voice made me suspect that the lady who faced me was not really angry at me. But, searching her face, I couldn't find the hint of a smile.

Embarrassed, my parents would regularly need to explain their children's inability to speak flowing Spanish during those years. My mother met the wrath of her brother, her only brother, when he came up from Mexico one summer with his family. He saw his nieces and nephews for the very first time. After listening to me, he looked away and said what a disgrace it was that I couldn't speak Spanish "*su proprio idioma.*" He made that remark to my mother; I noticed, however, that he stared at my father.

I clearly remember one other visitor from those years. A long-time friend of my father from San Francisco would come to stay with us for several days in late August. He took great interest in me after he realized that I couldn't answer his questions in Spanish. He would grab me as I started to leave the kitchen. He would ask me something. Usually he wouldn't bother to wait for my mumbled response. Knowingly, he'd murmur: "*¿Ay Pocho, Pocho, adónde vas?*" And he would press his thumbs into the upper part of my arms, making me squirm with currents of pain. Dumbly, I'd stand there, waiting for his wife to notice us, for her to call him off with a benign smile. I'd giggle, hoping to deflate the tension between us, pretending that I hadn't seen the glittering scorn in his glance.

I remember that man now, but seek no revenge in this telling. I recount such incidents only because they suggest the fierce power Spanish had for many people I met at home; the way Spanish was associated with closeness. Most of those people who called me a *pocho* could have spoken English to me. But they would not. They seemed to think that Spanish was the only language we could use, that Spanish alone permitted our close association. (Such persons are vulnerable always to the ghetto merchant and the politician who have learned the value of speaking their clients' family language to gain immediate trust.) For my part, I felt that I had somehow committed a sin of betrayal by learning English. But betrayal against whom? Not against visitors to the house exactly. No, I felt that I had betrayed my immediate family. I knew that my parents had encouraged me to learn English. I knew that I had turned to English only with angry reluctance. But once I spoke English with ease, I came to feel guilty. (This guilt defied logic.) I felt that I had shattered the intimate bond that had once held the family close. This original sin against my family told whenever anyone addressed me in Spanish and I responded, confounded.

But even during those years of guilt, I was coming to sense certain consoling truths about language and English. I remember playing with a friend in the backyard one day, when my grandmother appeared at the window. Her face was stern with suspicion when she saw the boy (the *gringo*) I was with. In Spanish she called out to me, sounding the whistle of her ancient breath. My companion looked up and watched her intently as she lowered the window and moved, still visible, behind the light curtain, watching us both. He wanted to know what she had said. I started to tell him, to say,—to translate her Spanish words into English. The problem was, however, that though I knew how to translate exactly *what* she had told me, I realized that any translation would distort the deepest meaning of her message: It had been directed only to me. This message of intimacy could never be translated because it was not *in* the words she had used but passed *through* them. So any translation would have seemed wrong; her words would have been stripped of an essential meaning. Finally, I decided not to tell my friend anything. I told him that I didn't hear all she had said.

This insight unfolded in time. Making more and more friends outside my house, I began to distinguish intimate voices speaking through *English*. I'd listen at times to a close friend's confidential tone of secretive whisper. Even more remarkable were those instances when, for no special reason apparently, I'd become conscious of the fact that my companion was speaking only to me. I'd marvel just hearing his voice. It was a stunning event: to be able to break through his words, to be able to hear this voice or the other, to realize that it was directed only to me. After such moments of intimacy outside the house, I began to trust hearing intimacy conveyed through my family's English. Voices at home at last punctured sad confusion. I'd hear myself addressed as an intimate at home once again. Such moments were never as raucous with sound as past times had been when we had had "private" Spanish to use. (Our English-sounding house was never to be as noisy as our Spanish-speaking house had been.) Intimate moments were usually soft moments of sounds. My mother was in the dining room while I did my homework nearby. And she looked over at me. Smiled. Said something—her words said nothing very important. But her voice sounded to tell me (*We are together.*) I was her son. . . .

Intimacy thus continued at home; intimacy was not stilled by English. It is true that I would never forget the great change of my life, the diminished occasions of intimacy. But there would also be times when I sensed the deepest truth about language and intimacy. *Intimacy is not created by a particular language; it is created by intimates.* The great change in my life was not linguistic but social. If, after becoming a successful student, I no longer heard intimate voices as often as I had earlier, it was not because I spoke English rather than Spanish. It was because I used public language for most of the day. I moved easily at last, a citizen in a crowded city of words. (1983, 28–32)

Questions for Writing and Discussion

1. Read the excerpt over and pick out important points to which you would like to respond. Try connecting the writer's ideas on intimacy with your own experience and observations. You may begin by questioning, comparing, criticizing, or interpreting. Remember to use specific language to explain and illustrate your ideas.
2. Discuss Rodriguez's ideas of private, or intimate, and public language. Point out the text that most aptly deals with the public and private identity, family identity, and school identity. In what other stories or experiences have you seen this kind of identity development?
3. How is the author's concept of family defined in the excerpt? What sort of relationship do you think he had with his mother? His grandmother? Other relatives?
4. Based on the preceding excerpt, what do you think Rodriguez's concept of "intimacy" is?

Student Writing Sample

Here is a sample of a journal entry, in response to question 1. Read it and respond to it, including how your own entry differs in content, style, or point of view.

While reading Rodriguez, I found myself reflecting back on my upbringing and my language education. My father was born in Montevideo, and the majority of my relatives are living in Montevideo or Santo Domingo, the Dominican Republic. My father left his family and moved to the U.S.A. and joined the army. When he became a citizen of the U.S.A., he shortened his last name in an effort to fit in better. He met my mother, a native from New Jersey from a Brazilian family, and they got married in the U.S.A. My mother made every effort to learn Spanish and traveled to South America to meet the family. His family was not accepting of her and has always made things difficult, though eventually somewhat friendly. When I was born, my father refused to speak Spanish to me initially. He spoke his English, which carried a heavy accent. When he used to call me at college, people would let me know that there was someone with a strong accent on the phone looking for me. I knew it was Dad. Eventually we did communicate in Spanish, Portuguese, and some French, which was his fourth language from having gone to school in France, but that was much later. It was my mother who made the effort to have my sister and me learn my father's language. Because I learned Spanish much later, when I was young the private and public language were the same with me—English.

I was born in the United States. We moved to Portugal when I was seven. I attended an American school which mandated 45 minutes of Portuguese a day, and later special classes, such as Art, Music, and Gym, that were also given in Portuguese. I learned Portuguese quickly, wanting to make friends and fit in. We had a maid who would not allow me to go into her kitchen until I spoke something in Portuguese to her. I remember resenting Spanish, the language of my father, when I initially moved to Portugal, probably because I wanted to master the Portuguese. Every Christmas season however, we would go to Spain to spend the holidays with my relatives, and though I never had any formal training in Spanish, I did learn to be fluent (though I never felt real secure with it). My cousins knew how I felt and would tease my pronunciation with certain words, which, of course, just made me feel less competent. We then returned to the United States.

I didn't realize until my mother's death what a strong part of my life Portuguese represented. At her funeral, I felt comforted by listening to the sounds of Portuguese around me . . . the English sounded cold to me. Perhaps it goes hand in hand with the culture that the language portrays, to me. Of course, this does not resemble everyone in the U.S. culture; after all I am married to a very "gringo" man and love him dearly. But on an overall view, I find the Latin cultures to be warmer, more family oriented, and more comforting. I will always feel more intimate, closer to a person when I speak Spanish or Portuguese.

Today, two years later, I really miss my conversations with my mother and the intimacy they held. When I communicate with my sister, we speak both languages, switching languages with the setting, the people, or the lack of a word in one language to the other. If I am upset about something, I would much prefer to speak to you about it in Spanish or Portuguese. I have kept in touch with friends from South America and Europe, and I feel a special bond with them by being able to communicate in Spanish or Portuguese. I was very happy recently when a new Spanish station started on the radio which played music in that language.

Student Writing Sample

Here is a sample response to question 4.

After reading the excerpt, I am reminded of how Richard Rodriguez's writing reminds me of my teenage diary in which my secrets and concerns were revealed to my private self. It was my private language, not intended for the public realm. His writing seems so personal, so organic.

One wonders how his life would have been different had he attended a school where Spanish was spoken? I think he would have been the good student he was; I also think that he would have been more comfortable with both his public and private selves.

The great lesson of school and of socialization is to gain a public identity and language. I think that the private belongs at home, at least for children. And, people need more than one language and mode of expression.

> Now that you have read these two responses to the Rodriguez excerpt, divide into small groups and discuss your responses.

Other Selves

Besides the language of the intimate, familiar and the public, official language, there are other languages and other identities. Rodriguez, a devout Catholic, enjoyed going to church to hear the liturgy in Latin, which he understood because of the similarity to Spanish. The Latin liturgy had a special significance for him that was different than the other two languages.

> Latin, the nuns taught us, was a universal language. One could go into a Catholic church anywhere in the world and hear the very same mass. But Latin was also a dead language, a tongue foreign to most Catholics. As an altar boy, I memorized Latin in blank envelopes of sound: *Ad day um qui lay tee fee cat u ven tu tem may um*. Many of the "ordinary" prayers of the mass were generally recognizable to me. (Any Catholic who used a bilingual missal could, after a while, recognize the meaning of whole prayers like the *Credo*.) I had the advantage of being able to hear in the shrouded gallery of Latin sounds echoes of Spanish words familiar to me. Listening to a priest I could often grasp the general sense of what he was saying—but I didn't always try to. In part, Latin permitted escape from the prosaic world. Latin's great theatrical charm, its sacred power, was that it could translate human aspiration to a holy tongue. The Latin mass, moreover, encouraged private reflection. The sounds of Latin would sometimes blur my attention to induce an aimless drift inward. But then I would be called back by the priest's voice ("*Oremus . . .*") to public prayer, the reminder that an individual has the aid of the Church in his life. I was relieved of the burden of being alone before God through my membership in the Church. (1983, 98–99)

In the previous excerpt, what purpose did Latin have for Rodriguez? Could it be said that a public and private self existed in Latin? Explain why or why not. Do you think the fact that the Spanish language is derived from Latin could partly explain Rodriguez's attraction to it?

The Film *Mi Familia*

The family is of central importance in the Latin cultures. Families will stay together throughout all kinds of acculturation crises. Sometimes, families will forgo job or education opportunities in order to keep the family together. On the other hand, it is the strength that being a part of a family brings to its members that helps them survive the difficulties of an alien environment. Yet the acculturation process puts a tremendous amount of stress on the family and its members.

The movie *Mi Familia,* written and directed by Gregory Nava (1995), traces several generations of a Mexican family whose migration to California began when that state was still part of Mexico. The film speaks to the central focus of the culture, the family unit, and how important it is to the survival of the Mexicans as an ethnic group, the largest in the United States.

In the following excerpt from the screenplay, Isabel, who has come into the United States illegally in order to avoid getting killed, is talking to Jimmy, who has agreed to marry her in order to make her "legal." As a little boy Jimmy saw his brother Chucho killed by the Los Angeles police. He tells Isabel how angry he has felt and how this anger has led him to get into trouble with the police, and serve jail time. In fact, anger and alienation are central themes of this movie, as well as in *El Norte* (1983), another of Nava's movies about immigrants.

Isabel

I go around this big city. Grandisima ciudad. I'm alone. No one will know. When I was little the soldiers came at night. They took my father out and killed him right there. Right there in front of me. I was a little girl, but I see everything. Then we come here and I have no time to be a child. I work, work, only work. And the family I stay with are happy. I see them. But it is their happiness, not mine. No one knows me.

Jimmy

I know you. [meaning I recognize you, understand you on a deep level]

The two fall in love, having found in common issues of identity that stem from feeling alienated and having to deal with identity, the stereotypes of the public identity, and the resulting anger. Indeed, anger, identity, and self-respect are all subthemes in this film, which focuses on the family as a cultural and universal unit.

Can you think of any other films that you have seen that have similar themes?

Take Jimmy's line "I know you" and expand on its meaning.

How do you think being an innocent observer of a violent act can affect children?

As a class, watch the movie *Mi Familia.* It is available at most video rental stores.

Questions for Writing and Discussion

After you have watched the movie *Mi Familia,* answer the following questions.

1. Discuss the main characters, settings, and central idea of *Mi Familia.* What message is the film portraying about the acculturation process?
2. What character in the film would have best understood the excerpts from *Hunger of Memory?*
3. Discuss the concept of public and private identity as seen in the characters' behaviors in the movie.
4. Each member of the Sanchez family coped with acculturation differently. Select two members and compare their development as they attempted to adjust to the American culture.
5. There is a scene in which Memo brings his fiancée home to meet his family, in which Anglo cultural characteristics clash with Chicano. Describe the cultural clash and explain why this conflict occurred. How could it have been avoided?

Student Writing Sample

Here is a sample response to question 2. See how it differs from what you wrote.

> In this movie, it is clear that the family is central to the emotional health of each of the characters. It is the center of everything, while the members revolve around it, like the spokes of a wheel. Jose felt his main job was to work hard for the good of the family. That is why he felt saddened by the death of his son Chucho and the disillusionment of his son Jimmy. Jimmy is distanced from the family by the death of his brother, but he finds redemption in the love of his son Carlitos. I liked the way Jimmy handled his son when he chopped down all the corn. In a wonderful metaphor, he described how the corn will go back to the earth to feed the rest of the corn. Even when the Sanchez family experienced loss, the experience brought them closer together. Despite all they suffered, we felt that Jimmy and Carlitos had an inseparable family bond.

Of all the characters of the film, I felt that Chucho and Paco had more in common with Rodriguez as he portrayed himself in *Hunger of Memory*. Chucho was rebellious and did not want to follow in his father's footsteps, much like Rodriguez, whose father chided him for being "a scholarship boy." Memo was the successful member of the family and had become a lawyer, marrying an Anglo girl. From the scene where he brought his wife home to meet his family, we get the impression that like Rodriguez, Memo has "sold out" and completely assimilated into the Anglo community. Like Rodriguez, he will suffer "hunger of memory" from the sacrifice of his roots.

The following is a review of the film *Mi Familia* by Roger Ebert, a well-known movie critic, from the *Chicago Sun Times:*

Through all the beauty, laughter and tears, the strong heart of the family beats, and everything leads up to a closing scene, between Jose and Marie, that is quite simple, joyous and heartbreaking. Rarely have I felt at the movies such a sense of time and history, of stories and lessons passing down the generations, of a family living in its memories.

Their story is the story of one Mexican-American family, but it is also in some ways the story of all families. Watching it, I was reminded of my own family's legends and heroes and stray sheep, and the strong sense of home. "Another country?" young Jose says, when he is told where Los Angeles is. "What does that mean—'another country'?" (Ebert 1995)

Do you agree with Roger Ebert? Tell why or why not and be specific in your explanation. Write your own critique of the film.

Questions for Writing and Discussion

1. The title of Rodriguez's book and the title of the film hold the key to the main concepts of each. Discuss the relationship between the main ideas of *Hunger of Memory* and *Mi Familia*.
2. Audiotape a 10-minute interview with a Mexican American or a member of another Latino group about his or her acculturation experience, particularly how it relates to language. In groups, play the tape and discuss what you learn. What new ideas did you learn about culture, acculturation, language, and identity?

3. Richard Rodriguez and Memo from the film were able to be more easily assimilated into the American culture than others were. Discuss why you think that this is so. Do you think they paid a price or made sacrifices to be successful? Did they have to evolve another identity, or could there have been another way?

4. Read this critical review of *Hunger of Memory* and respond by writing your own review of Rodriguez's book.

> As an eloquent and accomplished Mexican-American with impressive academic credentials, Rodriguez serves as a model and example of the triumph of the underprivileged individual. His success was achieved through individual and family effort, by overcoming his own past rather than through outside intervention of institutional and governmental supports. Many white readers, especially critics of bilingual education and affirmative action, have embraced him as their spokesperson and point to his rejection of these programs as proof of their worthlessness. (Roddenbury 1995, 429)

5. Write any question or comment that you might have for Richard Rodriguez or Gregory Nava.

6. Go to the library and research the topic of bilingual education. As a class, you may want to choose sides, pro and con, and debate the issue. Richard Rodriguez is an opponent of bilingual education. He feels that immigrants must learn the public language of English and be taught in that language if they are to hope to receive the same advantages as native English speakers (Rodriguez 1992, 19). Based on your research, can you think of reasons and strategies to counter his argument?

Chapter 3
Lost in Translation

Introduction

Being uprooted from one's culture can create a sense of loss in an individual, the loss of familiar surroundings. The comfort of familiarity is gone; everything is different—food, clothing, language, music, social gatherings. Feelings of loss are particularly acute when one is forced to migrate, such as in the cases of refugees or children who have no choice when parents migrate (Moghaddam, Taylor, and Wright 1993). In order to compensate, many strategies are used to deal with the sense of loss.

One of the strategies that an immigrant uses is the overidealization of the mother culture, while denigrating the new (Akhtar 1996, 1062). Sometimes the opposite strategy is employed, idealizing the new culture and denouncing everything reminiscent of the old. The goal, of course, should be eventually finding that "happy medium" in which one can integrate the two selves. A well-adjusted person is comfortable with both public and private, new and native identities, "owning" and admitting to both easily and freely, switching back and forth whenever appropriate. For example, one could talk in the native language to a compatriot of the native culture in line at the bank, but when it's time to talk to the teller, switch into standard English (the public language) with ease, and later meet another friend who likes to switch back and forth and talk in this code-switching manner. A well-integrated individual might acquaint those in his or her public domain, say, the workplace, with some aspects of his or her native or private identity, while using English from time to time at home, the private domain.

The degree to which the overidealization takes place in the psychological adjustment of an individual to the new culture will depend on, among other factors, if the individual had any choice in the decision to move to a new country. According to Akhtar, a noted psychologist and researcher, "Children are always exiled: they are not the ones who decide to leave and they cannot decide to return at will" (1996, 1064). Because they are wrenched from what is likely the only home they have known, children experience a profound sense of loss. Many who immigrate as children feel as if once the move occurred, their childhood was over, no matter what age they were. They therefore are prone to fantasizing about the landscape of the childhood as a kind of lost paradise.

Even though acquisition of a new culture and language can represent an opportunity to create a new self, it can also be an opportunity to further damage the already fragile self by a shattering of the internal world and the language that represents it. Denial and fragmentation of identity are potential negative responses to the individual's struggle to find a voice in the new home. The emotional homeostasis has been disturbed; the émigré feels hollow, unreal, as if he or she is playing a part in a play in which the identity of the audience is uncertain. In some situations, either the new or old self will dominate, suppressing the other identity. For children who are struggling to form an identity and sense of self, fragmentation is particularly destructive to their development.

Another common response to a new culture is detachment, avoiding becoming authentically involved with the new life in the new culture and intellectualizing the experience rather than processing it through the emotions. Other typical responses include overachievement, loss of confidence about one's appearance, extreme nostalgia for the home that was lost, and renunciation, a permanent sense of sadness and loss.

Questions for Writing and Discussion

1. Did you move from one place to another when you were a child? How did you feel? Tell about this experience. If you didn't, write about someone you know who did.

2. Do you know any children who immigrated to this country? What struggles did you observe that they encountered?

3. Why do you think children might have a tougher time coping with acculturation? Give an example if you can.

4. Do you know of any children who have managed to adjust in positive ways? Explain.

5. What are some of the ways that adults and older mentors can discover, monitor, and assist with adjustment issues that a newly emigrated child is encountering? You may want to conduct some research.

Eva Hoffman's *Lost in Translation*

Eva Hoffman migrated from Cracow, Poland, to Vancouver, British Columbia, at thirteen years of age. She speaks eloquently of her feelings of anomie, or loss of sense of self, in her book *Lost in Translation: A Life in a New Language* (1989). Almost overnight, Eva went from feeling like a pretty, self-assured young girl with many friends and a boyfriend, to feeling like an unattractive person who was alienated from her peers. The background for her carefree, happy young life had been the charming old European city of Cracow, a place that Eva loved and in which she felt safe. She was painfully wrenched away from this childhood haven, which she would always remember with *teknota,* or nostalgia.

In addition, she went from being part of a middle-class family with a live-in domestic worker to being quite poor, living in a basement in Vancouver that proved to be more expensive than the family had anticipated. But most important, Eva felt a loss of self, the self tied to the language of her girlhood. Her interior life continued to seem empty until she slowly began to learn English and learned to write her innermost thoughts in her diary in this new "public language." Eva, a gifted pianist, had contemplated becoming a concert pianist; she changed her career plans when she found that it was not considered a "serious" profession in the new world. Also gifted in language, she began to develop a voice in the new language. She struggled for authentic identity in this new mode of thinking and being. An introspective and sensitive person, Eva developed coping mechanisms, that of self-abnegation and renunciation and that of detachment. Suddenly in a lower social class she convinced herself she did not "need" material things. If she did not need them, she felt more complete.

Throughout all, her experience is infused with the sense of loss—the loss of her childhood self. Cracow is etched in her memory as a lovely mythical place in whose context she would have become someone totally different. Besides being from Poland, there is another facet of Eva's identity that she has to adjust to the North American culture—her identity as a Jew. As a child she learns from her parents that she has lost relatives in the Holocaust. It remains an evil specter that always is present in her subconscious, reminding her of the family tragedy, of her aunt Alina, her mother's sister, in the concentration camps. Her parents narrowly escaped a similar fate. In her recent book *Shtetl: The Life and Death of a Small Town and the World of Polish Jews* (1998), Hoffman further explores the complexities and ambiguities that lie in the Polish-Jewish relationships and the resulting hybrid identities.

Using the detachment that being an immigrant provides as an advantage in the American education system, her chosen career of writer and literary critic was enriched by her bicultural perspective. But years later, when she has become a successful writer and literary critic, Eva still feels a sense of loss that sometimes interferes with her relationships and her happiness, which is so eloquently articulated in *Lost in Translation*. The following excerpts will discuss the themes of learning a new voice, growing up as a teenager in a strange culture, ambition and the tendency to overachieve, feelings of detachment and self-denial, and adjustment to Jewish ethnicity in North America.

English: Both a Public and a Private Voice

Like Richard Rodriguez, Eva writes about her first attempts to find a voice in English. One opportunity came when her friend gave her a diary. In which language should she write? Eva made a critical choice. She wrote in the diary in her new language. Thus, she learned to develop English for both public and private uses.

For my birthday, Penny gives me a diary, complete with a little lock and key to keep what I write from the eyes of all intruders. It is that little lock—the visible symbol of the privacy in which the diary is meant to exist—that creates my dilemma. If I am indeed to write something entirely for myself, in what language do I write? Several times, I open the diary and close it again. I can't decide. Writing in Polish at this point would be a little like resorting to Latin or ancient Greek—an eccentric thing to do in a diary, in which you're supposed to set down your most immediate experiences and unpremeditated thoughts in the most unmediated language. Polish is becoming a dead language, the language of the untranslatable past. But writing for nobody's eyes in English? That's like doing a school exercise, or performing in front of yourself, a slightly perverse act of self-voyeurism.

Because I have to choose something, I finally choose English. If I am to write about the present, I have to write in the language of the present, even if it's not the language of the self. As a result, the diary becomes surely one of the more impersonal exercises of that sort produced by an adolescent girl. These are no sentimental effusions of rejected love, eruptions of familial anger, or consoling broodings about death. English is not the language of such emotions. Instead, I set down my reflections on the ugliness of wrestling; on the elegance of Mozart, and on how Dostoyevsky puts me in mind of El Greco. I write down Thoughts. I Write.

There is a certain pathos to this naive snobbery, for the diary is an earnest attempt to create a part of my persona that I imagine I would have grown into in Polish. In the solitude of this most private act, I write, in my public language, in order to update what might have been my other self. The diary is about me and not about me at all. But on one level, it allows me to make the first jump. I learn English through writing, and, in turn, writing gives me a written self. Refracted through the double distance of English and writing, this self—my English self—becomes oddly objective; more than anything, it perceives. It exists more easily in the abstract sphere of thoughts and observations than in the world. For a while, this impersonal self, this cultural negative capability, becomes the truest thing about me. When I write, I have a real existence that is proper to the activity of writing—an existence that takes place midway between me and the sphere of artifice, art, pure language. This language is beginning to invent another me. However, I discover something odd. It seems that when I write (or, for that matter, think) in English, I am unable to use the word "I." I do not go as far as the schizophrenic "she"—but I am driven, as by a compulsion, to the double, the Siamese-twin "you." (1989, 120–21)

Questions for Writing and Discussion

1. Other than in the choice of language, how is Eva's diary unlike what it might have been had she remained in Poland? How does language affect the subjects she chooses to write about?
2. What does Eva mean when she says her writing in the diary is about her and not about her at all?
3. Why does she have trouble writing the word "I"? Why do you think she uses "you" and not "she"?
4. What does Eva mean when she writes about her "English self." "It exists more easily in the abstract sphere of thoughts and observations than in the world." (121)?

Adolescence in a Strange City

In Poland, growing up as a little girl, Eva felt self-confident, loved, admired. When she came to North America as an adolescent girl with the characteristic consciousness about appearances, she had to make quite an adjustment to the social norms of style and dress. She recounts one episode when a family friend, Mrs. Lieberman, takes her into the bathroom and begins shaving her armpits without even asking her permission. Remembering another such episode, Eva writes:

> Mrs. Lieberman is among several Polish ladies who have been in Canada long enough to consider themselves well versed in native ways, and who seem to find me deficient in some quite fundamental respects. Since in Poland I was considered a pretty young girl, this requires a basic revision of my self image. But there's no doubt about it; after the passage across the Atlantic, I've emerged as less attractive, less graceful, less desirable. In fact, I can see in these women's eyes that I'm a somewhat pitiful specimen—pale, with thick eyebrows, and without any bounce in my hair, dressed in clothes that have nothing to do with the current fashion. And so they energetically set out to rectify these flaws. One of them spends a day with me, plucking my eyebrows and trying various shades of lipstick on my face. "If you were my daughter, you'd soon look like a princess," she says, thus implying an added deficiency in my mother. Another counselor takes me into her house for an evening, to initiate me into the mysteries of using shampoos and hair lotions, and putting my hair up in curlers; yet another outfits me with a crinoline and tells me that actually, I have a perfectly good figure—I just need to bring it out in the right ways. And several of them look at my breasts meaningfully, suggesting to my mother in an undertone that really, it's time I started wearing a bra. My mother obeys.
>
> I obey too, passively, mulishly, but I feel less agile and self-confident with every transformation. I hold my head rigidly, so that my precarious bouffant doesn't fall down, and I smile often, the way I see other girls do, though I'm careful not to open my lips too wide or bite them, so my lipstick won't get smudged. I don't know how to move easily in the high-heeled shoes somebody gave me.
>
> Inside its elaborate packaging, my body is stiff, sulky, wary. When I'm with my peers, who come in crinolines, lipstick, cars, and self-confidence naturally, my gestures show that I'm here provisionally, by

their grace, that I don't rightfully belong. My shoulders stoop, I nod frantically to indicate my agreement with others, I smile sweetly at people to show I mean well, and my chest recedes inward so that I don't take up too much space—mannerisms of a marginal, off-centered person who wants both to be taken in and to fend off the threatening others.

About a year after our arrival in Vancouver, someone takes a photograph of my family in their backyard, and looking at it, I reject the image it gives of myself categorically. This clumsy looking creature, with legs oddly turned in their high-heeled pumps, shoulders bent with the strain of resentment and ingratiation, is not myself. Alienation is beginning to be inscribed in my flesh and face. (1989, 109–10)

Questions for Writing and Discussion

1. Why do you think Eva feels less confident and agile with each change in her appearance?
2. Can you understand how someone can be attractive in one culture and awkward in another?

Immigrant Ambition: The Overachiever

Because Eva was a unique child, sensitive, complex, and precociously talented, she became ambitious, but not toward being a concert pianist as she had planned in Poland. Eva was amazed to find that a talent such as hers was not revered in Canada like it was in Poland, with its Old World values about art and music:

Immigrant energy, admirable name though it has gained for itself, does not seem a wholly joyful phenomenon to me. I understand the desperado drive that fuels it. But I also understand how it happens that so many immigrant Horatio Algers overshoot themselves so unexpectedly as they move on their sped-up trajectories through several strata of society all the way to the top. From the perspective outside, everything inside looks equally impenetrable, from below everything above equally forbidding. It takes the same bullish will to gain a foothold in some modest spot as to insist on entering some sacred inner sanctum, and that insistence, and ignorance, and obliviousness of the rules and social distinctions—not to speak of "your own place"—can land you anywhere at all. As a radically marginal person, you have two choices: to be intimidated by every situation, every social stratum, or to confront all of them with the same leveling vision, the same brash and stubborn spunk.

I, too, am goaded on by the forked whip of ambition and fear, and I derive a strange strength—a ferocity, a puissance—from the sense of my responsibility, the sense that survival is in my own hands. (1989, 157)

Eva was a talented classical pianist. This talent received much positive reinforcement in Poland. However, in Vancouver she finds a different response to her gift.

The only catch is that I have lost the sense of what, driven as I have become, I am driving toward. The patterns of my life have been so disrupted that I cannot find straight lines amid the disarray. Gradual change within one context, one diagram, is one thing; scrambling all the coordinates is another. "Being a pianist," for example, means something entirely different in my new cultural matrix. It is no longer the height of glamour or the heart of beauty. "What a nice tune," my friends say when I play a Beethoven sonata for them, but I see that they don't care. Moreover, Mrs. Steiner and others inform me, it's not a solid profession, and it will hardly assure my ability to support myself. "Where are you going to get the money for music lessons in New York?" somebody asks me. "A person in your position has to think practically." "You're too intelligent to become a musician," others tell me. But there is nothing in the world that takes a more incandescent intelligence, the intelligence of your whole being! I want to reply. (1989, 158)

Questions for Writing and Discussion

1. What are the two choices that Eva feels she must make with regard to ambition? Can you explain why you think she feels this way?
2. How do you think it made Eva feel to find her talent devalued in her new surroundings? Do you think it would have been different had she not met Mrs. Steiner and heard her opinion about being a musician?

Denunciation and Detachment

Among the many disruptions and changes in her situation, Eva had to cope with an apparent decline in social class. Her living standard in Cracow had been more middle class. Her coping mechanism once in Vancouver was to pull back, detach herself from what was happening around her, and acquire the objective viewpoint of an anthropologist, all the while romanticizing her earlier life in Poland. As a further coping strategy, she began to see herself as a somewhat tragic victim and became stoic, intellectualizing her experience:

> For a long time, confronting the danger both of self-division and of deprivation, I cultivate a rigorous renunciation. I suppose it serves me well. Like some visiting Indian swami, I learn to measure myself against no one and to feel at home everywhere. Not envying is the condition of my dignity, and I protect that dignity with my life. In a sense it is my life—the only base I have to stand on. If I sometimes have to go around with a run in my stocking when I am in college, if I can't afford the long trek home during Christmas recess, it doesn't matter. I have my essential humanity, that essential humanity which I learned to believe in as a Jewish girl in Poland and which I've now salvaged with the help of withdrawal and indifference. "Sometimes I see you with a steel rod running down the middle of your back," a friend once tells me. He sees more than most.
>
> My detachment would serve me even better if it were entirely genuine. It isn't. Underneath my carefully trained serenity, there is a cauldron of seething lost loves and a rage at the loss. And there is—for all that—a longing for a less strenuous way to maintain my identity and my pride. I want to gather experience with both my hands, not only with my soul. Essential humanity is all very well, but we need the colors of our time and the shelter of a specific place. (1989, 139)

Questions for Writing and Discussion

1. Why does Eva feel that her sense of detachment isn't real or genuine?
2. What does she mean by the "colors of our time and the shelter of a place"?

Triangulation of Experience

In her effort to cope with acquiring a new identity, Eva would triangulate her experiences. This means that when she felt overwhelmed by something in her new culture or country she would shift her perspective to another place and point in time. This helped her to gain objectivity and emotional distance:

> This is the point to which I have tried to triangulate, this private place, this unassimilable part of my self. . . . We all need to find this place in order to know that we exist not only within culture but also outside it. We need to triangulate to something—the past, the future, our own untamed perceptions, another place—if we're not to be subsumed by the temporal and temporary ideas of our time . . . finding such a point of calibration is particularly difficult now, when our collective air is oversaturated with trivial and important and contradictory and mutually canceling messages. And yet, I could not have found this true axis, could not have made my way through the maze, if I had not assimilated and mastered voices of my time and place—the only language through which we can learn to think and speak. The silence that comes out of articulateness is the inchoate and desperate silence of chaos. The silence that comes after words is the fullness from which the truth of our perceptions can crystallize. It's only after I've taken the disparate bits of cultural matter, after I've accepted its seductions and its snares, that I can make my way through the medium of language to distill my own meanings; and it's only coming from the ground up that I can hit the tenor of my own sensibility, hit home. (276)

Questions for Writing and Discussion

1. What is triangulation? Explain it in your own words. Why does Eva feel triangulation is good for everyone? How does it help her adjust?
2. Why does Eva feel the medium of language is so important to making her life meaningful?

Rooftops of Crakow. (Photography courtesy of Benjamin Rifkin with thanks to the Center for Russia, Eastern Europe, and Central Asia of the University of Wisconsin–Madison.)

Childhood Identity and Idealization of Home

The specific place that Eva had come from, Cracow, was very much woven within her childhood identity and perspectives. It is an ancient European city with a rich history and a vibrant artistic life. It has been called a "city which puts its faith in God and the graces, rather than politics" (Kostyal 1995).

> The rest of Cracow, the city of my daily life, is a place not of mystery but of secrets. Mystery only deepens as you go further into it, but secrets give themselves up unto the light. Cracow to me is a city of shimmering light and shadow, with the shadow only adding more brilliance to the patches of wind and sun. I walk the streets in a state of musing, anticipating pleasure. Its narrow byways, its echoing courtyards, its jewellike interiors are there for my delectation; they are there for me to get to know. . . .

The city is full of history, though I don't experience it as that. To me, it is natural that a city should be very old, that it should have cavelike cafes with marble-topped tables, medieval church spires, and low, Baroque arcades. Age is one of the things that encloses me with safety; Cracow has always existed, it's a given, it doesn't change much. It has layers and layers of reality. (1989, 38–39)

Questions for Writing and Discussion

1. Eva seems to find comfort in the age of Cracow. Why do you think this is? How does her age at immigration affect her memory of it?
2. Cracow is a beautiful old European city. Do you think Eva would have idealized it and felt such nostalgia when remembering it if it were not so different from Vancouver?
3. Can you remember any places you visited or lived in your childhood? How does your childhood memory represent them?

Being Jewish in North America

Cracow's charm is marred by the specter of Auschwitz, only 40 miles west of the city. Though she had a happy childhood in Cracow, Eva experienced anti-semitism from time to time: when she was teased by peers and when the political climate turned hostile in 1957 and Catholic prayer was instituted in schools. Eva's parents told her to stand proudly while avoiding being disrespectful, but not to say the Lord's Prayer.

Living under the shadow of the Holocaust profoundly affected Eva, who was very much in touch with her Jewish roots. She lived daily with the reality of the Holocaust because her mother's sister died in a concentration camp. But she found a different perspective on the Holocaust as an adult living in the United States:

A writer of my parents' generation who was himself in a concentration camp once told me that the Holocaust is the standard by which we should judge the world. But I think that the paradoxical task of my generation, caught within this awful story, is to get adjusted to the ordinary world in which we actually live, to acknowledge the reality given to us.

While my American friends, after undergoing the normal disillusionments of adult life, gradually temper their optimism, I try to slough off excess darkness that is false to my condition. Paradoxically, it's not an easy adjustment to make; our first knowledge is the most powerful, and the shadows cast by it upon the imagination can be more potent than the solid evidence of our own experience. (1989, 253)

Questions for Writing and Discussion

First, summarize Eva Hoffman's thoughts on each of the issues presented in the preceding excerpts. Then answer the following questions.

1. Do you feel that Eva is unique, or are there many Evas in our society? What can we learn from them about all children struggling to acculturate?
2. Do you think that the 1960s was a confusing time in which to emigrate to the United States? Do you think it is easier to emigrate to the U.S. now?
3. Do you think it would be easier or harder for gifted children to acculturate?
4. What problems can students have who are immigrants of Jewish heritage?
5. How were the strategies of detachment and triangulation useful to Eva? Do you know others who have used this perspective? Where are the advantages and disadvantages?
6. How can we help children, particularly those who emigrate at adolescence, acculturate to our society? Do you think it would be more difficult for girls or for boys? Explain your response.
7. What does Eva have in common with Richard Rodriguez? How does she feel about her public and private self?
8. We have mentioned a few of the more common responses to coping with acculturation: development of voice in the public language, detachment and renunciation, the need to overachieve, overidealization of the native culture, loss of confidence and self-esteem in physical appearance, the need to triangulate. What others can you think of?

Student Writing Samples

Here are sample writings that respond to questions 5 and 6. Compare them with your own and your classmates'.

I find the part about triangulation to be a fascinating way of talking about feeling detached, like an anthropologist feels when studying a new culture. I have felt that way myself at times when I have moved to Chicago from New York City with my family. It is as though you are on the outside looking in at a new world, a new context. When all seems so strange, it is hard to find meaning when you first enter a new situation. It feels like everything you say and do is forced.

And I felt very self-conscious, as if someone were looking at me. I remember going to a department store to buy a blouse. The salesgirl came up and I spoke so slowly that she completely misunderstood me. It was as though I was speaking a foreign language. In my mind, I kept shifting my perspective back to Puerto Rico and how I would have felt in a similar situation there.

Eva Hoffman's exact verbs and nouns used to connote her feelings back then are painfully disconcerting. They unveil themes of alienation, imprisonment, suffocation, a divided self, and unvented rage. For years, she didn't even have enough command of the language (never mind the sense of speaking amongst equals) to express her feelings or relax with a joke. Even her attempts to write in her diary were stifled by language. What language to use? The Polish she knew didn't seem to express this new land exactly, and she didn't know enough English to move it along with any of the wit and irony she could so easily let fly back home. At night, when language would have been there for her to sort her day, no words came.

A teenager, arriving on these shores, she found herself both drawing attention (for her newness and differences) as well as being shut out (knowing it was not her place to speak) for the very same reasons. The women who fluttered around her, treating her halfway between princess and Cinderella (before the ball), shaved her armpits, painted her face, chose her clothes, and taught her (by their mannerisms) not to take up much space. In essence, they robbed her of any dignity or sense of presence. In addition to this are those gaps created by language, history, geography, and culture.

I can relate to some of what she is saying. I don't think you have to arrive here from a distant shore to feel so distant from the artifice. I remember as a teen attending "make-out" parties where people were just supposed to casually "couple up" and "pucker up;" and all I wanted to do was "throw up." I stopped going but felt, because I couldn't go along, I just didn't belong.

When you march to your own drum, you stick out your chin and march along. My parents were raised in a New York City Italian ghetto. There it was easy to keep a number of the Italian values and customs and pieces of the language intact. Moving to the suburbs—where the ethnic and economic groups were mixed, the dialect absent, the perspective changed—was like moving to another country. My family's way was often not the *in* way, and learning to fit in was often accomplished with great difficulty.

Optional Activities

1. Interview someone whom you have met who is from Poland, if possible. Then transcribe parts of the tape that you find particularly interesting and share with the class.
2. Interview someone who is Jewish. What identities exist? What kinds of cultural awareness did you acquire that you did not have before?
3. Rent the film *Schindler's List* and watch it. Write a journal entry about the psychological realities that the protagonists encountered, both Schindler and the Jewish survivors.

Chapter 4
A Hybrid Feminine Voice

Introduction

In chapter 3, Eva Hoffman describes the problems of an adolescent when emigrating to another country. Teenagers can have a particularly difficult experience acclimating to the new environment. Because so many developmental changes are taking place, puberty is a fragile time, physically, emotionally, and mentally. Girls can have an especially difficult time; their sense of self is often distorted and confused. According to Carol Gilligan, a Harvard psychologist and coauthor of *At the Crossroads* (Gilligan and Brown 1992), girls who were self-assertive in early youth often lose their voices when they reach puberty, going inward, becoming wary of expressing their true feelings. Though her research was conducted in the United States, in private school, two of her subjects were from immigrant families. The same phenomenon was observed in the girls from other cultures as well as in the American-born girls. Gilligan says that girls need to have strong relationships with women to break false images of perfection and foster more realistic expectations for themselves, thus preventing unnecessary suffering and the resultant weak self-esteem (230). Immigrant girls, whose sense of self may already be fractured because of the move, particularly need strong feminine role models in the new culture.

Not all older women find it easy to "open up" and help young girls find their assertive voice. Corroborating the research findings of Gilligan, authors Belenky, Clinchy, Goldberger, and Tarule (1996) have investigated "women's way of knowing" and found that intuitive knowledge that women use as a preferred modality of learning is not often valued and nurtured in the academic and professional domains of society. Tending to prefer indirect styles of communication, women are sometimes misunderstood by men, who tend to prefer direct styles of communication, according to linguist Deborah Tannen's (1990) case study research. These gender issues, already heightened at puberty, make the demands of acculturation seem particularly difficult for the female teenaged immigrant. When most teenagers are asserting their independence, she cannot: she has no choice when her parents decide to immigrate. This lack of choice runs counter to the process of individuation that marks the adolescent, fostering instead a prolonged dependent stage because the young individual has to join the family in the acculturation efforts.

Julia Alvarez's *Something to Declare*

Like Eva Hoffman, Julia Alvarez had little choice in the decision to emigrate to the United States. She came to the United States when her family was forced into exile because of the persecution of dissenters by the Trujillo regime in the Dominican Republic. She found that it was very difficult to make the transition because at that time there were not as many Dominicans living in New York City as there are now. She remembers being called a "spic" and "Chiquita Banana" once listeners discerned her accent.

As a young girl coming of age, she had to struggle to find her voice in her native culture; in the Dominican family, machismo is the norm and girls are meant for domesticity and maternity. In contrast, when she came to the United States, she discovered that American girls had more freedom and opportunity to shape their own futures.

In the following excerpt, "I Want to Be Miss America," from *Something to Declare* (1998) Julia and her sisters are measuring themselves against the contestants in the pageant, which was popular in the 1960s as something young American women should aspire to.

I Want to Be Miss America

As young teenagers in our new country, my three sisters and I searched for clues on how to look as if we belonged here. We collected magazines, studied our classmates and our new TV, which was where we discovered the Miss America contest.

Watching the pageant became an annual event in our family. Once a year, we all plopped down in our parents' bedroom, with Mami and Papi presiding from their bed. In our nightgowns, we watched the fifty young women who had the American look we longed for.

The beginning was always the best part—all fifty contestants came on for one and only one appearance. In alphabetical order, they stepped forward and enthusiastically introduced themselves by name and state. "Hi! I'm! Susie! Martin! Miss! Alaska!" Their voices rang with false cheer. You could hear, not far off, years of high-school cheerleading, pom-poms, bleachers full of moon-eyed boys, and moms on the phones, signing them up for all manner of lessons and making dentist appointments.

There they stood, fifty puzzle pieces forming the pretty face of America, so we thought, though most of the color had been left out, except for one, or possibly two, light-skinned black girls. If there was a "Hispanic," she usually looked all-American, and only the last name, López or Rodríguez, often mispronounced, showed a trace of a great-great-grandfather with a dark, curled mustache and a sombrero charging the Alamo. During the initial roll-call, what most amazed us was that some contestants were ever picked in the first place. There were homely girls with cross-eyed smiles or chipmunk cheeks. My mother would inevitably shake her head and say, "The truth is, these Americans believe in democracy—even in looks."

We were beginning to feel at home. Our acute homesickness had passed, and now we were like people recovered from a shipwreck, looking around at our new country, glad to be here. "I want to be in America," my mother hummed after we'd gone to see *West Side Story*, and her four daughters chorused, "OK by me in America." We bought a house in Queens, New York, in a neighborhood that was mostly German and Irish, where we were the only "Hispanics." Actually, no one ever called us that. Our teachers and classmates at the local Catholic schools referred to us as "Porto Ricans" or "Spanish." No one knew where the Dominican Republic was on the map. "South of Florida," I explained, "in the same general vicinity as Bermuda and Jamaica." I could just as well have said west of Puerto Rico or east of Cuba or right next to Haiti, but I wanted us to sound like a vacation spot, not a Third World country, a place they would look down on.

Although we wanted to look like we belonged here, the four sisters, our looks didn't seem to fit in. We complained about how short we were, about how our hair frizzed, how our figures didn't curve like those of the bathing beauties we'd seen on TV.

"The grass always grows on the other side of the fence," my mother scolded. Her daughters looked fine just the way they were.

But how could we trust her opinion about what looked good when she couldn't even get the sayings of our new country right? No, we knew better. We would have to translate our looks into English, iron and tweeze them out, straighten them, mold them into Made-in-the-U.S.A. beauty.

So we painstakingly rolled our long, curly hair round and round, using our heads as giant rollers, ironing it until we had long, shining shanks, like our classmates and the contestants, only darker. Our skin was diagnosed by beauty consultants in department stores as sallow; we definitely needed a strong foundation to tone down that olive. We wore tights even in the summer to hide the legs Mami would not let us shave. We begged for permission, dreaming of the contestants' long, silky limbs. We were ten, fourteen, fifteen, and sixteen—merely children, Mami explained. We had long lives ahead of us in which to shave.

We defied her. Giggly and red-faced, we all pitched in to buy a big tube of Nair at the local drugstore. We acted as if we were purchasing contraceptives. That night we crowded into the bathroom, and I, the most courageous along these lines, offered one of my legs as a guinea pig. When it didn't become gangrenous or fall off as Mami had predicted, we creamed the other seven legs. We beamed at each other; we were one step closer to that runway, those flashing cameras, those oohs and aahs from the audience.

Mami didn't even notice our Naired legs; she was too busy disapproving of the other changes. Our clothes, for one. "You're going to wear *that* in public!" She'd gawk, as if to say, What will the Americans think of us?

"This *is* what the Americans wear," we would argue back.

But the dresses we had picked out made us look cheap, she said, like bad, fast girls—gringas without *vergüenza*, without shame. She preferred her choices: fuchsia skirts with matching vests, flowered dresses with bows at the neck or gathers where you wanted to look slim, everything bright and busy, like something someone might wear in a foreign country.

Our father didn't really notice our new look at all but, if called upon to comment, would say absently that we looked beautiful. "Like Marilina Monroe." Still, during the pageant, he would offer insights into what he thought made a winner. "Personality, Mami," my father would say from his post at the head of the bed, "Personality is the key," though his favorite contestants, whom he always championed in the name of personality, tended to be the fuller girls with big breasts who gushed shamelessly at Bert Parks. "Ay, Papi," we would groan, rolling our eyes at each other. Sometimes, as the girl sashayed back down the aisle, Papi would break out in a little Dominican song that he sang whenever a girl had a lot of swing in her walk:

Yo no tumbo caña,
Que la tumba el viento,
Que la tumba Dora
Con su movimiento!

[I don't have to cut the cane,
the wind knocks it down,
The wind of Dora's movement
As she walks downtown.]

My father would stop on a New York City street when a young woman swung by and sing this song out loud to the great embarrassment of his daughters. We were sure that one day when we weren't around to make him look like the respectable father of four girls, he would be arrested.

My mother never seemed to have a favorite contestant. She was an ex-beauty herself, and no one seemed to measure up to her high standards. She liked the good girls who had common sense and talked about their education and about how they owed everything to their mothers. "Tell that to my daughters," my mother would address the screen, as if none of us were there to hear her. If we challenged her—how exactly did we *not* appreciate her?—she'd maintain a wounded silence for the rest of the evening. Until the very end of the show, that is, when all our disagreements were forgotten and we waited anxiously to see which of the two finalists holding hands on that near-empty stage would be the next reigning queen of beauty. How can they hold hands? I always wondered. Don't they secretly wish the other person would, well, die?

My sisters and I always had plenty of commentary on all the contestants. We were hardly strangers to this ritual of picking the beauty. In our own family, we had a running competition as to who was the prettiest of the four girls. We coveted one another's best feature: the oldest's dark, almond shaped eyes, the youngest's great mane of hair, the third oldest's height and figure. I didn't have a preferred feature, but I was often voted the cutest, though my oldest sister liked to remind me that I had the kind of looks that wouldn't age well. Although she was only eleven months older than I was, she seemed years older, ages wiser. She bragged about the new kind of math she was learning in high school, called algebra, which she said I would never be able to figure out. I believed her. Dumb and ex-cute, that's what I would grow up to be.

As for the prettiest Miss America, we sisters kept our choices secret until the very end. The range was limited—pretty white women who all *really* wanted to be wives and mothers. But even the small and inane set of options these girls represented seemed boundless compared with what we were used to. We were being groomed to go from being dutiful daughters to being dutiful wives with hymens intact. No stops along the way that might endanger the latter; no careers, no colleges, no shared apartments with girlfriends, no boyfriends, no social lives. But the young women on-screen, who were being held up as models in this new country, were in college, or at least headed there. They wanted to do this, they were going to do that with their lives. Everything in our native culture had instructed us otherwise: girls were to have no aspirations beyond being good wives and mothers.

Sometimes she would even be a contestant headed for law school or medical school. "I wouldn't mind having an office visit with her," my father would say, smirking. The women who caught my attention were the prodigies who bounded onstage and danced to tapes of themselves playing original compositions on the piano, always dressed in costumes they had sewn, with a backdrop of easels holding paintings they'd painted. "Overkill," my older sister insisted. But if one good thing came out of our watching this yearly parade of American beauties, it was that subtle permission we all felt as a family: a girl could excel outside the home and still be a winner.

Every year, the queen came down the runway in her long gown with a sash like an old-world general's belt of ammunition. Down the walkway she paraded, smiling and waving while Bert sang his sappy song that made our eyes fill with tears. When she stopped at the very end of the stage and the camera zoomed in on her misty-eyed beauty and the credits began to appear on the screen, I always felt let down. I knew I would never be one of those girls, ever. It wasn't just the blond, blue-eyed looks or the beautiful, leggy figure. It was who she was—an American—and we were not. We were foreigners, dark-haired and dark-eyed with olive skin that could never, no matter the sun blocks or foundation makeup, be made into peaches and cream.

Had we been able to see the future, beyond our noses, which we thought weren't the right shape; beyond our curly hair, which we wanted to be straight; and beyond the screen, which inspired us with a limited vision of what was considered beautiful in America, we would have been able to see the late sixties coming. Soon, ethnic looks would be in. Even Barbie, that quintessential white girl, would suddenly be available in different shades of skin color with bright, colorful outfits that looked like the ones that Mami had picked out for us. Our classmates in college wore long braids like Native Americans and embroidered shawls and peasant blouses from South America, and long, diaphanous skirts and dangly earrings from India. They wanted to look exotic—they wanted to look like us.

We felt then a gratifying sense of inclusion, but it had unfortunately come too late. We had already acquired the habit of doubting ourselves as well as the place we came from. To this day, after three decades of living in America, I feel like a stranger in what I now consider my own country. I am still the young teenager sitting in front of the black-and-white TV in my parents' bedroom, knowing in my bones I will never be the beauty queen. There she is, Miss America, but even in my up-to-date, enlightened dreams, she never wears my face. (1998, 37–44)

Questions for Writing and Discussion

1. Why do you think that Julia wanted the Dominican Republic to be thought of as a "vacation spot"?
2. How do you think she felt when people thought she was a "Porto Rican"? Why did she feel her looks had to be "translated into American"?
3. Why was there such a fascination in her family with the Miss America pageant?
4. What does the author mean by the following observation: "If there was a 'Hispanic,' she usually looked all-American, and only the last name, López or Rodríguez, often mispronounced, showed a trace of a great-great-grandfather with a dark, curled mustache and a sombrero charging the Alamo." (38)
5. What did her parents feel about the attempts that Julia and her siblings made to "fit in" by making changes in their appearance, including the clothes they bought?
6. To what extent are attitudes toward features like body hair determined by culture? Why do you think that the Alvarez girls had to sneak around to use Nair?
7. To what extent, unconsciously perhaps, was the contest reinforcing Julia's aspirations as a writer?

8. What does Julia mean that in the 1960s "ethnic looks were in"? You may want to research the 1960s and the styles of clothing that were popular.
9. Why do you think the "Miss America" pageant has become less popular in American culture than it used to be?

Women as Mentors

When girls are able to find their voice and stay strong in identity, it is often due to relationships with their mothers or some other older female role model. In Gilligan and Brown's study of adolescent girls, *At the Crossroads* (1992), Carol Gilligan interviewed Nawal, a teenager who had immigrated with her family from the Middle East. Gilligan found that Nawal depended on her relationship with her mother to help her deal with her physical appearance, which was different from others in her class.

> Okay, my Mom has black, curly wild hair, really dark skin. Dresses like, she wears a huge silver earring, does not fit the stereotypical Laurel mother image, does not. This is a woman who comes in from the senior luncheon and she says, "Nawal, am I dressed okay?" . . . and her hair was down and curly and she had enormous earrings, huge necklace, this black kind of fitted sundress thing, sandals, a lot of jewelry, and everyone was staring. . . . And I love the way she dresses, and I love the fact that she is different . . . but when I was younger, it use to bother me, and I hated being Arabic. I hated being different, and I hated having an Arabic name. And I was really almost embarrassed by my Mom. (Gilligan and Brown 1992, 225)

When Nawal's mother asked her, "Do you really want me to look like everyone else?" Nawal thought and decided that she wouldn't like that. This was an important step for her. Nawal devoted her senior speech to this subject; in the school's open assembly she voiced her resistance to American standards of beauty—the standards that led Nawal, a dark-skinned Arabic young woman, to wish for long, long blond hair and blue eyes and to judge herself and her mother as ugly or not beautiful.

In addition to Nawal, Gilligan found many girls who have been at odds with American standards of beauty and who felt victimized by stereotyping. Because these girls are more vulnerable and at risk, they benefit from close relationships with their mothers or an older female mentor. They are able to find security by listening to older women in their communities and learning how to question the accepted norms not only in beauty but in everyday life.

Women play an important role in helping girls find their true identity, by allowing girls to get close to them while still retaining their authority status. This is by no means easy, and some teachers or mentors are uncomfortable, afraid of revealing too much of themselves and losing control. Gilligan and Brown's study also found that male teachers can serve as mentors to girls. In fact, many girls preferred men as teachers because some men were able to be more themselves with the girls in their classes; whereas women were more guarded (226). Women who are teachers or mentors may need to find ways to be more open with girls.

Questions for Writing and Discussion

1. What ideas in the passage by Nawal summarize Gilligan's point about relationships among women, girls, and their self-esteem?
2. Can you connect these ideas with something that has happened in your own experience or observations?
3. How does culture intensify what girls experience?
4. If Eva Hoffman could have a communication with Nawal, what would they say to one another?

Communication and Gender

Females' experiences of immigration are affected also by general issues of communication style. Research by linguists on the topic of communication and gender in the United States has found that while women tend to speak up more in general in conversations, men tend to set the agenda by giving opinions, suggestions, and information, while women tend to react. Body language is different also; women tend to gather themselves in, and men tend to stretch out. Men tend to spend a lot of time sizing each other up while women tend to seek closeness by self-revelation, with the goal of networking relationships.

Though both attempt to establish relationships, men tend to seek a hierarchy that concerns power and their positions. Women, on the other hand, tend to be interested in their positions, not so much with respect to hierarchy, but rather their positions in the network of relationships. The result of these differing goals is different ways of speaking (Tannen 1990), with women tending toward indirect communication and men toward direct communication.

Similarly, different cultures value different styles of communication. The use of the indirect style of communication is often evident among both women and men in other cultures. Most Americans assume that a direct, say-what-you-mean style is more effective. However, other cultures do not find this to be the case. For example, according to research by Tannen (1994), for the Japanese, a person who is in power (usually male) has the option to be direct or indirect when making a demand on a person in an inferior social position. According to anthropologist Takie Sugiyama, Japanese culture places a high value on *omoiyai*, which is translated as "empathy." A person should be able to sense another person's intent and feelings intuitively. For this reason, Japanese people put a high value on the ability to communicate indirectly (Tannen 1994, 96).

Tannen offers (in translation) the example of an exchange that took place when the boss of a photography store in Japan wanted a female worker to find a store that would make a black-and-white print from a color print:

> On this matter, that-that—on the leaflet? This photo, I am thinking of changing it to black-and-white and making it clearer. . . . I went to a photo shop and asked them. They said they didn't do monochrome. I asked if they knew any place that did. They said they didn't know. They weren't very helpful, but anyway, a place must be found, the negative brought to it, and the picture developed. (Tannen 1994, 85)

The boss had the choice of using direct communication to show his power or indirect communication in order to build trust and rapport in the relationship. In addition, indirect is often used to show the power to choose the style of communication. This is like when an executive goes to work in informal attire. He or she can choose this kind of self-presentation because of his or her position. This is not to say that those who give commands to subordinates in a direct manner are all insecure and ineffectual, but to emphasize that speaking indirectly may not reveal insecurity on the part of the speaker, but a concern with building rapport and appearing accessible to a person of inferior position (Tannen 1994, 96).

In another cultural context, Tannen found that Greeks and Americans interpret conversations differently. A Greek is far more likely to interpret a question as an indirect way of making a request. For example a person could say "Do you want to have a meeting about this?" and to a Greek person, this means, "I want to have a meeting about this" (Tannen 1994, 104).

In my own experience in the community college ESL classroom, I have found that students from Puerto Rican and Dominican cultures tend not to want to make a request directly. They say they feel it is rude and disrespectful. Rather, they get together as a group and select someone they feel can indirectly make their feelings known. This person will approach me and say something like, "There are some people who are wondering. . . ." The person with the complaint is never mentioned.

Questions for Writing and Discussion

1. Can you think of examples of direct and indirect styles of communication? If possible, relate your examples to culture, class, or gender.
2. Interview someone from another culture about when they feel they use a direct or an indirect style of communication.
3. Do you think that women use the indirect style of communication universally or depending on the cultural context? Please explain and give specific examples.
4. Can you think of ways we as educators can help girls learn to use both styles of communication effectively? Do you think that boys communicate in a different style than girls?

Optional Writing and Discussion Exercises

1. Interview a young female teenager who has recently come from another culture. Ask her about female stereotypes in this culture and gender relationships in her culture.
2. Read the play *A Doll's House* by Henrik Ibsen and examine its relationships. Are there any symmetrical ones? Asymmetrical ones?
3. Rent the video *Nine to Five*. Watch it and discuss the relationships. How does the protagonist change with regard to her identity and voice?

Chapter 5
Immigration and the Generation Gap

Introduction

Immigrants who come to the United States often have to deal with two distinct and dissonant problems. One of these is how to acculturate and adjust to a foreign culture, which is often itself in a state of flux; the other is how to deal with older relatives who still identify with the traditions of the native culture while only paying lip service to the new one. Sociolinguists tell us that the first-born generation in the United States tends to embrace the new culture, while the subsequent generations are nostalgic and longingly looking for their roots.

The first-born children and their mothers in Amy Tan's novel *The Joy Luck Club* explore these issues in a dramatic way. The "aunties" and mothers represent the older generation and their values. They have suffered in China, and while they are glad to give their daughters the opportunity to have a better life in America, they do not want to lose them to the new culture's ways. They want their daughters to continue many of the "old" Chinese traditions, thereby keeping them close. The children are affected as well by the ambiguity in their parents.

A conflict can arise in children whose parents are adhering to traditions from the native culture, which can result in resistance to learning anything new. According to Nieto's (1996, 392) resistance theory, children will resist learning, either actively or passively, due to a number of cultural or linguistic misperceptions. One misperception is that the assigned schoolwork is meaningless to the child's real world and therefore not worth doing. The result can affect school performance in a variety of ways, from children forgetting to do homework to dropping out of school altogether.

Questions for Writing and Discussion

1. If you can, describe your own relationship with your mother.
2. What have you learned about your background or your native culture from your mother?
3. How do you think your generation is different from your mother's?

Amy Tan's *The Joy Luck Club*

Amy Tan was born in Oakland, California, in the 1950s, to parents who had immigrated from China. She did not go to China until 1987, but when she did she felt an immediate affinity with the country and its culture. Though her parents wanted her to be a neurosurgeon or a concert pianist, she became a teacher of disabled children instead. Later, she took up writing.

The Joy Luck Club, her first book, alternates between the stories of the older generation of women, whom she called the "aunties," in China in the 1940s before the diaspora and those of their American-born daughters. The first excerpt, "Without Wood," describes the relationship between mother An-Mei Hsu and daughter Rose Hsu Jordan. The second excerpt, "Two Kinds," describes the relationship between mother Suyuan Woo and daughter Jing-Mei "June" Woo.

Rose Hsu Jordan

Without Wood

I used to believe everything my mother said, even when I didn't know what she meant. Once when I was little, she told me she knew it would rain because lost ghosts were circling near our windows, calling "Woo-woo" to be let in. She said doors would unlock themselves in the middle of the night unless we checked twice. She said a mirror could see only my face, but she could see me inside out even when I was not in the room.

And all these things seemed true to me. The power of her words was that strong.

She said that if I listened to her, later I would know what she knew: where true words came from, always from up high, above everything else. And if I didn't listen to her, she said my ear would bend too easily to other people, all saying words that had no lasting meaning, because they came from the bottom of their hearts, where their own desires lived, a place where I could not belong.

The words my mother spoke did come from up high. As I recall, I was always looking up at her face as I lay on my pillow. In those days my sisters and I all slept in the same double bed. Janice, my oldest sister, had an allergy that made one nostril sing like a bird at night, so we called her Whistling Nose. Ruth was Ugly Foot because she could spread her toes out in the shape of a witch's claw. I was Scaredy Eyes because I would squeeze shut my eyes so I wouldn't have to see the dark, which Janice and Ruth said was a dumb thing to do. During those early years, I was the last to fall asleep. I clung to the bed, refusing to leave this world for dreams.

"Your sisters have already gone to see Old Mr. Chou," my mother would whisper in Chinese. According to my mother, Old Mr. Chou was the guardian of a door that opened into dreams. "Are you ready to go see Old Mr. Chou, too?" And every night I would shake my head.

"Old Mr. Chou takes me to bad places," I cried.

Old Mr. Chou took my sisters to sleep. They never remembered anything from the night before. But Old Mr. Chou would swing the door wide open for me, and as I tried to walk in, he would slam it fast, hoping to squash me like a fly. That's why I would always dart back into wakefulness.

But eventually Old Mr. Chou would get tired and leave the door unwatched. The bed would grow heavy at the top and slowly tilt. And I would slide headfirst, in through Old Mr. Chou's door, and land in a house without doors or windows.

I remember one time I dreamt of falling through a hole in Old Mr. Chou's floor. I found myself in a nighttime garden and Old Mr. Chou was shouting, "Who's in my backyard?" I ran away. Soon I found myself stomping on plants with veins of blood, running through fields of snapdragons that changed colors like stoplights, until I came to a giant playground filled with row after row of square sandboxes. In each sandbox was a new doll. And my mother, who was not there but could see me inside out, told Old Mr. Chou she knew which doll I would pick. So I decided to pick one that was entirely different.

"Stop her! Stop her!" cried my mother. As I tried to run away, Old Mr. Chou chased me, shouting, "See what happens when you don't listen to your mother!" And I became paralyzed, too scared to move in any direction.

The next morning, I told my mother what happened, and she laughed and said, "Don't pay attention to Old Mr. Chou. He is only a dream. You only have to listen to me."

And I cried, "But Old Mr. Chou listens to you too."

More than thirty years later, my mother was still trying to make me listen. A month after I told her that Ted and I were getting a divorce, I met her at church, at the funeral of China Mary, a wonderful ninety-two-year-old woman who had played godmother to every child who passed through the doors of the First Chinese Baptist Church.

"You are getting too thin," my mother said in her pained voice when I sat down next to her. "You must eat more."

"I'm fine," I said, and I smiled for proof. "And besides, wasn't it you who said my clothes were always too tight?"

"Eat more," she insisted, and then she nudged me with a little spiral-bound book hand-titled "Cooking the Chinese Way by China Mary Chan." They were selling them at the door, only five dollars each, to raise money for the Refugee Scholarship Fund.

The organ music stopped and the minister cleared his throat. He was not the regular pastor; I recognized him as Wing, a boy who used to steal baseball cards with my brother Luke. Only later Wing went to divinity school, thanks to China Mary, and Luke went to the county jail for selling stolen car stereos.

"I can still hear her voice," Wing said to the mourners. "She said God made me with all the right ingredients, so it'd be a shame if I burned in hell."

"Already cre-*mated*," my mother whispered matter-of-factly, nodding toward the altar, where a framed color photo of China Mary stood. I held my finger to my lips the way librarians do, but she didn't get it.

"That one, we bought it." She was pointing to a large spray of yellow chrysanthemums and red roses. "Thirty-four dollars. All artificial, so it will last forever. You can pay me later. Janice and Matthew also chip in some. You have money?"

"Yes, Ted sent me a check."

Then the minister asked everyone to bow in prayer. My mother was quiet at last, dabbing her nose with Kleenex while the minister talked: "I can just see her now, wowing the angels with her Chinese cooking and gung-ho attitude."

And when heads lifted, everyone rose to sing hymn number 335, China Mary's favorite: "You can be an-gel, ev-ery day on earth. . . "

But my mother was not singing. She was staring at me.

"Why does he send you a check?" I kept looking at the hymnal, singing: "Sending rays of sun-shine, full of joy from birth."

And so she grimly answered her own question: "He is doing monkey business with someone else."

Monkey business? Ted? I wanted to laugh—her choice of words, but also the idea! Cool, silent, hairless Ted, whose breathing pattern didn't alter one bit in the height of passion? I could just see him, grunting "Ooh-ooh-ooh" while scratching his armpits, then bouncing and shrieking across the mattress trying to grab a breast.

"No, I don't think so," I said.

"Why not?"

"I don't think we should talk about Ted now, not here."

"Why can you talk about this with a psyche-atric and not with mother?"

"Psychiatrist."

"Psyche-atricks," she corrected herself.

"A mother is best. A mother knows what is inside you," she said above the singing voices. "A psyche-atricks will only make you *hulihudu*, make you see *heimongmong*."

Back home, I thought about what she said. And it was true. Lately I had been feeling *hulihudu*. And everything around me seemed to be *heimongmong*. These were words I had never thought about in English terms. I suppose the closest in meaning would be "confused" and "dark fog."

But really, the words mean much more than that. Maybe they can't be easily translated because they refer to a sensation that only Chinese people have, as if you were falling headfirst through Old Mr. Chou's door, then trying to find your way back. But you're so scared you can't open your eyes, so you get on your hands and knees and grope in the dark, listening for voices to tell you which way to go.

I had been talking to too many people, my friends, everybody it seems, except Ted. To each person I told a different story. Yet each version was true, I was certain of it, at least at the moment that I told it.

To my friend Waverly, I said I never knew how much I loved Ted until I saw how much he could hurt me. I felt such pain, literally a *physi-*

cal pain, as if someone had torn off both my arms without anesthesia, without sewing me back up.

"Have you ever had them torn off *with* anesthesia? God! I've never seen you so hysterical," said Waverly. "You want my opinion, you're better off without him. It hurts only because it's taken you fifteen years to see what an emotional wimp he is. Listen, I know what it feels like."

To my friend Lena, I said I was better off without Ted. After the initial shock, I realized I didn't miss him at all. I just missed the way I felt when I was with him.

"Which was what?" Lena gasped. "You were depressed. You were manipulated into thinking you were nothing next to him. And now you think you're nothing without him. If I were you, I'd get the name of a good lawyer and go for everything you can. Get even."

I told my psychiatrist I was obsessed with revenge. I dreamt of calling Ted up and inviting him to dinner, to one of those trendy who's-who places, like Café Majestic or Rosalie's. And after he started the first course and was nice and relaxed, I would say, "It's not that easy, Ted." From my purse I would take out a voodoo doll which Lena had already lent me from her props department. I would aim my escargot fork at a strategic spot on the voodoo doll and I would say, out loud, in front of all the fashionable restaurant patrons. "Ted, you're such an impotent bastard and I'm going to make sure you stay that way." *Wham!*

Saying this, I felt I had raced to the top of a big turning point in my life, a new me after just two weeks of psychotherapy. But my psychiatrist just looked bored, his hand still propped under his chin. "It seems you've been experiencing some very powerful feelings," he said sleepy-eyed. "I think we should think about them more next week."

And so I didn't know what to think anymore. For the next few weeks, I inventoried my life, going from room to room trying to remember the history of everything in the house: things I had collected before I met Ted (the hand-blown glasses, the macramé wall hangings, and the rocker I had recaned); things we bought together right after we were married (most of the big furniture); things people gave us (the glass-domed clock that no longer worked, three sake sets, four teapots); things he picked out (the signed lithographs, none of them beyond number twenty-five in a series of two hundred fifty, the Steuben crystal strawberries); and things I picked out because I couldn't bear to see them left behind (the mismatched candlestick holders from garage sales, an antique quilt with a hole in it, odd-shaped vials that once contained ointments, spices, and perfumes).

I had started to inventory the bookshelves when I got a letter from Ted, a note actually, written hurriedly in ballpoint on his prescription notepad. "Sign 4x where indicated," it read. And then in fountain-pen blue ink, "enc: check, to tide you over until settlement."

The note was clipped to our divorce papers, along with a check for ten thousand dollars, signed in the same fountain-pen blue ink on the note. And instead of being grateful, I was hurt.

Why had he sent the check with the papers? Why the two different pens? Was the check an afterthought? How long had he sat in his office determining how much money was enough? And why had he chosen to sign it with *that* pen?

I still remember the look on his face last year when he carefully undid the gold foil wrap, the surprise in his eyes as he slowly examined every angle of the pen by the light of the Christmas tree. He kissed my forehead. "I'll use it only to sign important things," he had promised me.

Remembering that, holding the check, all I could do was sit on the edge of the couch feeling my head getting heavy at the top. I stared at the x's on the divorce papers, the wording on the prescription notepad, the two colors of ink, the date of the check, the careful way in which he wrote, "Ten thousand only and no cents."

I sat there quietly, trying to listen to my heart, to make the right decision. But then I realized I didn't know what the choices were. And so I put the papers and the check away, in a drawer where I kept store coupons which I never threw away and which I never used either.

My mother once told me why I was so confused all the time. She said I was without wood. Born without wood so that I listened to too many people. She knew this, because once she had almost become this way.

"A girl is like a young tree," she said. "You must stand tall and listen to your mother standing next to you. That is the only way to grow strong and straight. But if you bend to listen to other people, you will grow crooked and weak. You will fall to the ground with the first strong wind. And then you will be like a weed, growing wild in any direction, running along the ground until someone pulls you out and throws you away."

But by the time she told me this, it was too late. I had already begun to bend. I had started going to school, where a teacher named Mrs. Berry lined us up and marched us in and out of rooms, up and down hallways while she called out, "Boys and girls, follow me." And if you didn't listen to her, she would make you bend over and whack you with a yardstick ten times.

I still listened to my mother, but I also learned how to let her words blow through me. And sometimes I filled my mind with other people's thoughts—all in English—so that when she looked at me inside out, she would be confused by what she saw.

Over the years, I learned to choose from the best opinions. Chinese people had Chinese opinions. American people had American opinions. And in almost every case, the American version was much better.

It was only later that I discovered there was a serious flaw with the American version. There were too many choices, so it was easy to get confused and pick the wrong thing. That's how I felt about my situation with Ted. There was so much to think about, so much to decide. Each decision meant a turn in another direction.

The check, for example, I wondered if Ted was really trying to trick me, to get me to admit that I was giving up, that I wouldn't fight the divorce. And if I cashed it, he might later say the amount was the whole settlement. Then I got a little sentimental and imagined, only for a moment, that he had sent me ten thousand dollars because he truly loved me; he was telling me in his own way how much I meant to him. Until I realized that ten thousand dollars was nothing to him, that I was nothing to him.

I thought about putting an end to this torture and signing the divorce papers. And I was just about to take the papers out of the coupon drawer when I remembered the house.

I thought to myself, I love this house. The big oak door that opens into a foyer filled with stained-glass windows. The sunlight in the breakfast room, the south view of the city from the front parlor. The herb and flower garden Ted had planted. He used to work in the garden every weekend, kneeling on a green rubber pad, obsessively inspecting every leaf as if he were manicuring fingernails. He assigned plants to certain planter boxes. Tulips could not be mixed with perennials. A cutting of aloe vera that Lena gave me did not belong because we had no other succulents.

I looked out the window and saw the calla lilies had fallen and turned brown, the daisies had been crushed down by their own weight, the lettuce gone to seed. Runner weeds were growing between the flagstone walkways that wound between the planter boxes. The whole thing had grown wild from months of neglect.

And seeing the garden in this forgotten condition reminded me of something I once read in a fortune cookie: When a husband stops paying attention to the garden, he's thinking of pulling up roots. When was the last time Ted pruned the rosemary back? When was the last time he squirted Snail B-Gone around the flower beds?

I quickly walked down to the garden shed, looking for pesticides and weed killer, as if the amount left in the bottle, the expiration date, anything would give me some idea of what was happening in my life. And then I put the bottle down. I had the sense someone was watching me and laughing.

I went back in the house, this time to call a lawyer. But as I started to dial, I became confused. I put the receiver down. What could I say? What did I want from divorce—when I never knew what I wanted from marriage?

The next morning, I was still thinking about my marriage; fifteen years of living in Ted's shadow. I lay in bed, my eyes squeezed shut, unable to make the simplest decisions.

I stayed in bed for three days, getting up only to go to the bathroom or to heat up another can of chicken noodle soup. But mostly I slept. I took the sleeping pills Ted had left behind in the medicine cabinet. And for the first time I can recall, I had no dreams. All I could remember was falling smoothly into a dark space with no feeling of dimension or direction. I was the only person in this blackness. And every time I woke up, I took another pill and went back to this place.

But on the fourth day, I had a nightmare. In the dark, I couldn't see Old Mr. Chou, but he said he would find me, and when he did, he would squish me into the ground. He was sounding a bell, and the louder the bell rang the closer he was to finding me. I held my breath to keep from screaming, but the bell got louder and louder until I burst awake.

It was the phone. It must have rung for an hour nonstop. I picked it up.

"Now that you are up, I am bringing you leftover dishes," said my mother. She sounded as if she could see me now. But the room was dark, the curtains closed tight.

"Ma, I can't . . . " I said. "I can't see you now. I'm busy."

"Too busy for mother?"

"I have an appointment . . . with my psychiatrist."

She was quiet for a while. "Why do you not speak up for yourself?" she finally said in her pained voice. "Why can you not talk to your husband?"

"Ma," I said, feeling drained. "Please. Don't tell me to save my marriage anymore. It's hard enough as it is."

"I am not telling you to save your marriage," she protested. "I only say you should speak up."

When I hung up, the phone rang again. It was my psychiatrist's receptionist. I had missed my appointment that morning, as well as two days ago. Did I want to reschedule? I said I would look at my schedule and call back.

And five minutes later the phone rang again.

"Where've you been?" It was Ted.

I began to shake. "Out," I said.

"I've been trying to reach you for the last three days. I even called the phone company to check the line."

And I knew he had done that, not out of any concern for me, but because when he wants something, he gets impatient and irrational about people who make him wait.

"You know it's been two weeks," he said with obvious irritation.

"Two weeks?"

"You haven't cashed the check or returned the papers. I wanted to be nice about this, Rose. I can get someone to officially serve the papers, you know."

"You can?"

And then without missing a beat, he proceeded to say what he really wanted, which was more despicable than all the terrible things I had imagined.

He wanted the papers returned, signed. He wanted the house. He wanted the whole thing to be over as soon as possible. Because he wanted to get married again, to someone else.

Before I could stop myself, I gasped. "You mean you *were* doing monkey business with someone else?" I was so humiliated I almost started to cry.

And then for the first time in months, after being in limbo all that time, everything stopped. All the questions: gone. There were no choices. I had an empty feeling—and I felt free, wild. From high inside my head I could hear someone laughing.

"What's so funny?" said Ted angrily.

"Sorry," I said. "It's just that . . ." and I was trying hard to stifle my giggles, but one of them escaped through my nose with a snort, which made me laugh more. And then Ted's silence made me laugh even harder.

I was still gasping when I tried to begin again in a more even voice. "Listen, Ted, sorry . . . I think the best thing is for you to come over after work." I didn't know why I said that, but I felt right saying it.

"There's nothing to talk about, Rose."

"I know," I said in a voice so calmed it surprised even me. "I just want to show you something. And don't worry, you'll get your papers. Believe me."

I had no plan. I didn't know what I would say to him later. I knew only that I wanted Ted to see me one more time before the divorce.

What I ended up showing him was the garden. By the time he arrived, the late-afternoon fog had already blown in. I had the divorce papers in the pocket of my windbreaker. Ted was shivering in his sports jacket as he surveyed the damage to the garden.

"What a mess," I heard him mutter to himself, trying to shake his pant leg loose of a blackberry vine that had meandered onto the walkway. And I knew he was calculating how long it would take to get the place back into order.

"I like it this way," I said, patting the tops of the overgrown carrots, their orange heads pushing through the earth as if about to be born. And then I saw the weeds: Some had sprouted in and out of the cracks in the patio. Others had anchored on the side of the house. And even more had found refuge under loose shingles and were on their way to climbing up to the roof. No way to pull them out once they've buried themselves in the masonry; you'd end up pulling the whole building down.

Ted was picking up plums from the ground and tossing them over the fence into the neighbor's yard. "Where are the papers?" he finally said.

I handed them to him and he stuffed them in the inside pocket of his jacket. He faced me and I saw his eyes, the look I had once mistaken for kindness and protection. "You don't have to move out right away," he said. "I know you'll want at least a month to find a place."

"I've already found a place," I said quickly, because right then I knew where I was going to live. His eyebrows raised in surprise and he smiled—for the briefest moment—until I said, "Here."

"What's that?" he said sharply. His eyebrows were still up, but now there was no smile.

"I said I'm staying here," I announced again.

"Who says?" He folded his arms across his chest, squinted his eyes, examining my face as if he knew it would crack at any moment. That expression of his used to terrify me into stammers.

Now I felt nothing, no fear, no anger. "I say I'm staying, and my lawyer will too, once we serve you the papers," I said.

Ted pulled out the divorce papers and stared at them. His x's were still there, the blanks were still blank. "What do you think you're doing? Exactly what?" he said.

And the answer, the one that was important above everything else, ran through my body and fell from my lips: "You can't just pull me out of your life and throw me away."

I saw what I wanted: his eyes, confused, then scared. He was *hulihudu*. The power of my words was that strong.

✧ ✧ ✧

That night I dreamt I was wandering through the garden. The trees and bushes were covered with mist. And then I spotted Old Mr. Chou and my mother off in a distance, their busy movements swirling the fog around them. They were bending over one of the planter boxes.

"There she is!" cried my mother. Old Mr. Chou smiled at me and waved. I walked up to my mother and saw that she was hovering over something, as if she were tending a baby.

"See," she said, beaming, "I have just planted them this morning, some for you, some for me."

And below the *heimongmong*, all along the ground, were weeds already spilling out over the edges, running wild in every direction. (1989b, 206–20)

Questions for Writing and Discussion

1. Why do you think the chapter is entitled "Without Wood"?
2. What is the significance of *hulihudu* in this chapter? In what contexts does it occur?

3. Who is Mr. Chou? What does he represent?
4. What is the flaw in the "American version," as opposed to the Chinese version?
5. Explain Rose's dream at the end of the chapter.
6. How did Rose's mother influence her? How did her mother influence her mistakes and her successes?

Jing-Mei Woo
Two Kinds

My mother believed you could be anything you wanted to be in America. You could open a restaurant. You could work for the government and get good retirement. You could buy a house with almost no money down. You could become rich. You could become instantly famous.

"Of course you can be prodigy, too," my mother told me when I was nine. "You can be best anything. What does Auntie Lindo know? Her daughter, she is only best tricky."

America was where all my mother's hopes lay. She had come here in 1949 after losing everything in China: her mother and father, her family home, her first husband, and two daughters, twin baby girls. But she never looked back with regret. There were so many ways for things to get better.

We didn't immediately pick the right kind of prodigy. At first my mother thought I could be a Chinese Shirley Temple. We'd watch Shirley's old movies on TV as though they were training films. My mother would poke my arm and say, *"Ni kan"* — You watch. And I would see Shirley tapping her feet, or singing a sailor song, or pursing her lips into a very round O while saying, "Oh my goodness."

"Ni kan," said my mother as Shirley's eyes flooded with tears. "You already know how. Don't need talent for crying!"

Soon after my mother got this idea about Shirley Temple, she took me to a beauty training school in the Mission district and put me in the hands of a student who could barely hold the scissors without shaking. Instead of getting big fat curls, I emerged with an uneven mass of crinkly black fuzz. My mother dragged me off to the bathroom and tried to wet down my hair.

"You look like Negro Chinese," she lamented, as if I had done this on purpose.

The instructor of the beauty training school had to lop off these soggy clumps to make my hair even again. "Peter Pan is very popular these days," the instructor assured my mother. I now had hair the length of a boy's, with straight-across bangs that hung at a slant two inches above my eyebrows. I liked the haircut and it made me actually look forward to my future fame.

In fact, in the beginning, I was just as excited as my mother, maybe even more so. I pictured this prodigy part of me as many different images, trying each one on for size. I was a dainty ballerina girl standing by the curtains, waiting to hear the right music that would send me floating on my tiptoes. I was like the Christ child lifted out of the straw manger, crying with holy indignity. I was Cinderella stepping from her pumpkin carriage with sparkly cartoon music filling the air.

In all of my imaginings, I was filled with a sense that I would soon become *perfect*. My mother and father would adore me. I would be beyond reproach. I would never feel the need to sulk for anything.

But sometimes the prodigy in me became impatient. "If you don't hurry up and get me out of here, I'm disappearing for good," it warned. "And then you'll always be nothing."

✧ ✧ ✧

Every night after dinner, my mother and I would sit at the Formica kitchen table. She would present new tests, taking her examples from stories of amazing children she had read in *Ripley's Believe It or Not,* or *Good Housekeeping, Reader's Digest,* and a dozen other magazines she kept in a pile in our bathroom. My mother got these magazines from people whose houses she cleaned. And since she cleaned many houses each week, we had a great assortment. She would look through them all, searching for stories about remarkable children.

The first night she brought out a story about a three-year-old boy who knew the capitals of all the states and even most of the European countries. A teacher was quoted as saying the little boy could also pronounce the names of foreign cities correctly.

"What's the capital of Finland?" my mother asked me, looking at the magazine story.

All I knew was the capital of California, because Sacramento was the name of the street we lived on in Chinatown. "Nairobi!" I guessed, saying the most foreign word I could think of. She checked to see if that was possibly one way to pronounce "Helsinki" before showing me the answer.

The tests got harder—multiplying numbers in my head, finding the queen of hearts in a deck of cards, trying to stand on my head without using my hands, predicting the daily temperatures in Los Angeles, New York, and London.

One night I had to look at a page from the Bible for three minutes and then report everything I could remember. "Now Jehoshaphat had riches and honor in abundance and . . . that's all I remember, Ma," I said.

And after seeing my mother's disappointed face once again, something inside of me began to die. I hated the tests, the raised hopes and failed expectations. Before going to bed that night, I looked in the mirror above the bathroom sink and when I saw only my face staring back—and that it would always be this ordinary face—I began to cry. Such a sad, ugly girl! I made high-pitched noises like a crazed animal, trying to scratch out the face in the mirror.

And then I saw what seemed to be the prodigy side of me—because I had never seen that face before. I looked at my reflection, blinking so I could see more clearly. The girl staring back at me was angry, powerful. This girl and I were the same. I had new thoughts, willful thoughts, or rather thoughts filled with lots of won'ts. I won't let her change me, I promised myself. I won't be what I'm not.

So now on nights when my mother presented her tests, I performed listlessly, my head propped on one arm. I pretended to be bored. And I was. I got so bored I started counting the bellows of the foghorns out on the bay while my mother drilled me in other areas. The sound was comforting and reminded me of the cow jumping over the moon. And the next day, I played a game with myself, seeing if my mother would give up on me before eight bellows. After a while I usually counted only one, maybe two bellows at most. At last she was beginning to give up hope.

✧ ✧ ✧

Two or three months had gone without any mention of my being a prodigy again. And then one day my mother was watching *The Ed Sullivan Show* on TV. The TV was old and the sound kept shorting out.

Every time my mother got halfway up from the sofa to adjust the set, the sound would go back on and Ed would be talking. As soon as she sat down, Ed would go silent again. She got up, the TV broke into loud piano music. She sat down. Silence. Up and down, back and forth, quiet and loud. It was like a stiff embraceless dance between her and the TV set. Finally she stood by the set with her hand on the sound dial.

She seemed entranced by the music, a little frenzied piano piece with this mesmerizing quality, sort of quick passages and then teasing lilting ones before it returned to the quick playful parts.

"*Ni kan,*" my mother said, calling me over with hurried hand gestures. " Look here."

I could see why my mother was fascinated by the music. It was being pounded by a little Chinese girl, about nine years old, with a Peter Pan haircut. The girl had the sauciness of a Shirley Temple. She was proudly modest like a proper Chinese child. And she also did the fancy sweep of a curtsy, so that the fluffy skirt of her white dress cascaded slowly to the floor like the petals of a large carnation.

In spite of these warning signs, I wasn't worried. Our family had no piano and we couldn't afford to buy one, let alone reams of sheet music and piano lessons. So I could be generous in my comments when my mother bad-mouthed the little girl on TV.

"Play note right, but doesn't sound good! No singing sound," complained my mother.

"What are you picking on her for?" I said carelessly. "She's pretty good. Maybe she's not the best, but she's trying hard." I knew almost immediately I would be sorry I said that.

"Just like you," she said. "Not the best. Because you not trying." She gave me a little huff as she let go of the sound dial and sat down on the sofa.

The little Chinese girl sat down also to play an encore of "Anitra's Dance" by Grieg. I remember the song, because later on I had to learn how to play it.

✧ ✧ ✧

Three days after watching *The Ed Sullivan Show,* my mother told me what my schedule would be for piano lessons and piano practice. She had talked to Mr. Chong, who lived on the first floor of our apartment building. Mr. Chong was a retired piano teacher and my mother had traded house cleaning services for weekly lessons and a piano for me to practice on every day, two hours a day, from four until six.

When my mother told me this, I felt as though I had been sent to hell. I whined and then kicked my foot a little when I couldn't stand it anymore.

"Why don't you like me the way I am? I'm *not* a genius! I can't play the piano. And even if I could, I wouldn't go on TV if you paid me a million dollars!" I cried.

My mother slapped me. "Who ask you be genius?" she shouted. "Only ask you be your best. For you sake. You think I want you be genius? Hnnh! What for! Who ask you!"

"So ungrateful," I heard her mutter in Chinese. "If she had as much talent as she has temper, she would be famous now."

Mr. Chong, whom I secretly nicknamed Old Chong, was very strange, always tapping his fingers to the silent music of an invisible orchestra. He looked ancient in my eyes. He had lost most of his hair on top of his head and he wore thick glasses and had eyes that always looked tired and sleepy. But he must have been younger than I thought, since he lived with his mother and was not yet married.

I met the Old Lady Chong once and that was enough. She had this peculiar smell like a baby that had done something in its pants. And her fingers felt like a dead person's, like an old peach I once found in the back of the refrigerator; the skin just slid off the meat when I picked it up.

I soon found out why Old Chong had retired from teaching piano. He was deaf. "Like Beethoven!" he shouted to me. "We're both listening only in our head!" And he would start to conduct his frantic silent sonatas.

Our lessons went like this. He would open the book and point to different things, explaining their purpose: "Key! Treble! Bass! No sharps or flats! So this C major! Listen now and play after me!"

And then he would play the C scale a few times, a simple chord, and then, as if inspired by an old, unreachable itch, he gradually added more notes and running trills and a pounding bass until the music was really something quite grand.

I would play after him, the simple scale, the simple chord, and then I just played some nonsense that sounded like a cat running up and down on top of garbage cans. Old Chong smiled and applauded and then said, "Very good! But now you must learn to keep time!"

So that's how I discovered that Old Chong's eyes were too slow to keep up with the wrong notes I was playing. He went through the motions in half-time. To help me keep rhythm, he stood behind me, pushing down on my right shoulder for every beat. He balanced pennies on top of my wrists so I would keep them still as I slowly played scales and arpeggios. He had me curve my hand around an apple and keep that shape when playing chords. He marched stiffly to show me how to make each finger dance up and down, staccato like an obedient little soldier.

He taught me all these things, and that was how I also learned I could be lazy and get away with mistakes, lots of mistakes. If I hit the wrong notes because I hadn't practiced enough, I never corrected myself. I just kept playing in rhythm. And Old Chong kept conducting his own private reverie.

So maybe I never really gave myself a fair chance. I did pick up the basics pretty quickly, and I might have become a good pianist at that young age. But I was so determined not to try, not to be anybody different that I learned to play only the most ear-splitting preludes, the most discordant hymns.

Over the next year, I practiced like this, dutifully in my own way. And then one day I heard my mother and her friend Lindo Jong both talking in a loud bragging tone of voice so others could hear. It was after church, and I was leaning against the brick wall wearing a dress with stiff white petticoats. Auntie Lindo's daughter, Waverly, who was about my age, was standing farther down the wall about five feet away. We had grown up together and shared all the closeness of two sisters squabbling over crayons and dolls. In other words, for the most part, we hated each other. I thought she was snotty. Waverly Jong had gained a certain amount of fame as "Chinatown's Littlest Chinese Chess Champion."

"She bring home too many trophy," lamented Auntie Lindo that Sunday. "All day she play chess. All day I have no time do nothing but dust off her winnings." She threw a scolding look at Waverly, who pretended not to see her.

"You lucky you don't have this problem," said Auntie Lindo with a sigh to my mother.

And my mother squared her shoulders and bragged: "Our problem worser than yours. If we ask Jing-mei wash dish, she hear nothing but music. It's like you can't stop this natural talent."

And right then, I was determined to put a stop to her foolish pride.

✧ ✧ ✧

A few weeks later, Old Chong and my mother conspired to have me play in a talent show which would be held in the church hall. By then, my parents had saved up enough to buy me a secondhand piano, a black Wurlitzer spinet with a scarred bench. It was the showpiece of our living room.

For the talent show, I was to play a piece called "Pleading Child" from Schumann's *Scenes from Childhood.* It was a simple, moody piece that sounded more difficult than it was. I was supposed to memorize the whole thing, playing the repeat parts twice to make the piece sound longer. But I dawdled over it, playing a few bars and then cheating, looking up to see what I was playing. I daydreamed about being some-where else, about being someone else.

The part I liked to practice best was the fancy curtsy: right foot out, touch the rose on the carpet with a pointed foot, sweep to the side, left leg bends, look up and smile.

My parents invited all the couples from the Joy Luck Club to witness my debut. Auntie Lindo and Uncle Tin were there. Waverly and her two older brothers had also come. The first two rows were filled with chil-dren both younger and older than I was. The littlest ones got to go first. They recited simple nursery rhymes, squawked out tunes on miniature violins, twirled Hula Hoops, pranced in pink ballet tutus, and when they bowed or curtsied, the audience would sigh in unison, "Awww," and then clap enthusiastically.

When my turn came, I was very confident. I remember my childish excitement. It was as if I knew, without a doubt, that the prodigy side of me really did exist. I had no fear whatsoever, no nervousness. I re-member thinking to myself, This is it! This is it! I looked out over the audience, at my mother's blank face, my father's yawn, Auntie Lindo's stiff-lipped smile, Waverly's sulky expression. I had on a white dress layered with sheets of lace, and a pink bow in my Peter Pan haircut. As I sat down I envisioned people jumping to their feet and Ed Sullivan rushing up to introduce me to everyone on TV.

And I started to play. It was beautiful. I was so caught up in how lovely I looked that at first I didn't worry how I would sound. So it was a surprise to me when I hit the first wrong note and I realized something didn't sound quite right. And then I hit another and another followed that. A chill started at the top of my head and began to trickle down. Yet I couldn't stop playing, as though my hands were bewitched. I kept thinking my fingers would adjust themselves back, like a train switching to the right track. I played this strange jumble through two repeats, the sour notes staying with me all the way to the end.

When I stood up, I discovered my legs were shaking. Maybe I had just been nervous and the audience, like Old Chong, had seen me go through the right motions and had not heard anything wrong at all. I swept my right foot out, went down on my knee, looked up and smiled. The room was quiet, except for Old Chong, who was beaming and shouting, "Bravo! Bravo! Well done!" But then I saw my mother's face, her stricken face. The audience clapped weakly, and as I walked back to my chair, with my whole face quivering as I tried not to cry, I heard a little boy whisper loudly to his mother, "That was awful," and the mother whispered back, "Well, she certainly tried."

And now I realized how many people were in the audience, the whole world it seemed. I was aware of eyes burning into my back. I felt the shame of my mother and father as they sat stiffly throughout the rest of the show.

We could have escaped during intermission. Pride and some strange sense of honor must have anchored my parents to their chairs. And so we watched it all: the eighteen-year-old boy with a fake mustache who did a magic show and juggled flaming hoops while riding a unicycle. The breasted girl with white makeup who sang from *Madam Butterfly* and got honorable mention. And the eleven-year-old boy who won first prize playing a tricky violin song that sounded like a busy bee.

After the show, the Hsus, the Jongs, and the St. Clairs from the Joy Luck Club came up to my mother and father.

"Lots of talented kids," Auntie Lindo said vaguely, smiling broadly.

"That was somethin' else," said my father, and I wondered if he was referring to me a humorous way, or whether he even remembered what I had done

Waverly looked at me and shrugged her shoulders. "You aren't a genius like me," she said matter-of-factly. And if I hadn't felt so bad, I would have pulled her braids and punched her stomach.

But my mother's expression was what devastated me: a quiet, blank look that said she had lost everything. I felt the same way, and it seemed as if everybody were now coming up, like gawkers at the scene of an accident, to see what parts were actually missing. When we got on the bus to go home, my father was humming the busy-bee tune and my mother was silent. I kept thinking she wanted to wait until we got home before shouting at me. But when my father unlocked the door to our apartment, my mother walked in and then went to the back, into the bedroom. No accusations. No blame. And in a way, I felt disappointed. I had been waiting for her to start shouting, so I could shout back and cry and blame her for all my misery.

❖ ❖ ❖

I assumed my talent show fiasco meant I never had to play the piano again. But two days later, after school, my mother came out of the kitchen and saw me watching TV.

"Four clock," she reminded me as if it were any other day. I was stunned, as though she were asking me to go through the talent-show torture again. I wedged myself more tightly in front of the TV.

"Turn off TV," she called from the kitchen five minutes later.

I didn't budge. And then I decided. I didn't have to do what my mother said anymore. I wasn't her slave. This wasn't China. I had listened to her before and look what happened. She was the stupid one.

She came out from the kitchen and stood in the arched entryway of the living room. "Four clock," she said once again, louder.

"I'm not going to play anymore," I said nonchalantly. "Why should I? I'm not a genius."

She walked over and stood in front of the TV. I saw her chest was heaving up and down in an angry way.

"No!" I said, and I now felt stronger, as if my true self had finally emerged. So this was what had been inside me all along.

"No! I won't!" I screamed.

She yanked me by the arm, pulled me off the floor, snapped off the TV. She was frighteningly strong, half pulling, half carrying me toward the piano as I kicked the throw rugs under my feet. She lifted me up and onto the hard bench. I was heaving even more and her mouth was open, smiling crazily as if she were pleased I was crying.

"You want me to be someone that I'm not!" I sobbed. "I'll never be the kind of daughter you want me to be!"

"Only two kinds of daughters," she shouted in Chinese. "Those who are obedient and those who follow their own mind! Only one kind of daughter can live in this house. Obedient daughter!"

"Then I wish I wasn't your daughter. I wish you weren't my mother," I shouted. As I said these things I got scared. I felt like worms and toads and slimy things were crawling out of my chest, but it also felt good, as if this awful side of me had surfaced, at last.

"Too late change this," said my mother shrilly.

And I could sense her anger rising to its breaking point. I wanted to see it spill over. And that's when I remembered the babies she had lost in China, the ones we never talked about. "Then I wish I'd never been born!" I shouted. "I wish I were dead! Like them."

It was as if I had said the magic words. Alakazam!—and her face went blank, her mouth closed, her arms went slack, and she backed out of the room, stunned, as if she were blowing away like a small brown leaf, thin brittle lifeless.

It was not the only disappointment my mother felt in me. In the years that followed, I failed her so many times, each time asserting my own will, my right to fall short of expectations. I didn't get straight As. I didn't become class president. I didn't get into Stanford. I dropped out of college.

For unlike my mother, I did not believe I could be anything I wanted to be. I could only be me.

And for all those years, we never talked about the disaster at the recital or my terrible accusations afterward at the piano bench. All that remained unchecked, like a betrayal that was now unspeakable. So I never found a way to ask her why she had hoped for something so large that failure was inevitable.

And even worse, I never asked her what frightened me the most: Why had she given up hope?

For after our struggle at the piano, she never mentioned my playing again. The lessons stopped. The lid to the piano was closed, shutting out the dust, my misery, and her dreams.

So she surprised me. A few years ago, she offered to give me the piano, for my thirtieth birthday. I had not played in all those years. I saw the offer as a sign of forgiveness, a tremendous burden removed.

"Are you sure?" I asked shyly. "I mean, won't you and Dad miss it?"

"No, this is your piano," she said firmly. "Always your piano. You only one can play."

"Well, I probably can't play anymore," I said. "It's been years."

"You pick up fast," said my mother, as if she knew this was certain. "You have natural talent. You could been genius if you want to."

"No I couldn't."

"You just not trying," said my mother. And she was neither angry nor sad. She said it as if to announce a fact that could never be disproved. "Take it," she said.

But I didn't at first. It was enough that she had offered it to me. And after that, every time I saw it in my parents' living room, standing in front of the bay windows, it made me feel proud, as if it were a shiny trophy I had won back.

Last week I sent a tuner over to my parents' apartment and had the piano reconditioned, for purely sentimental reasons. My mother had died a few months before and I had been getting things in order for my father, a little bit at a time. I put the jewelry in special silk pouches. The sweaters she had knitted in yellow, pink, and bright orange—all the colors I hated—I put those in moth-proof boxes. I found some old Chinese silk dresses, the kind with little slits up the sides. I rubbed the old silk against my skin, then wrapped them in tissue and decided to take them home with me.

After I had the piano tuned, I opened the lid and touched the keys. It sounded even richer than I remembered. Really, it was a very good piano. Inside the bench were the same exercise notes with handwritten scales, the same secondhand music books with their covers held together with yellow tape.

I opened up the Schumann book to the dark little piece I had played at the recital. It was on the left-hand side of the page, "Pleading Child." It looked more difficult than I remembered. I played a few bars, surprised at how easily the notes came back to me.

And for the first time, or so it seemed, I noticed the piece on the right-hand side. It was called "Perfectly Contented." I tried to play this one as well. It had a lighter melody but the same flowing rhythm and turned out to be quite easy. "Pleading Child" was shorter but slower; "Perfectly Contented" was longer but faster. And after I played them both a few times, I realized they were two halves of the same song. (1989a, 141–55)

Questions for Writing and Discussion

1. How did her mother's wishing that her daughter would become a prodigy influence Jing-Mei Woo's thoughts while she was growing up?
2. Based on what you know of her mother, why do you think Jing-Mei's mother wanted her to be a prodigy?
3. Why was Jing-Mei so angry?
4. When the recital ended, what devastated Jing-Mei most?
5. Describe the differences between mother and daughter, citing the passages that helped you see the differences.
6. Why do you think the chapter was called "Two Kinds"?

Student Writing Sample

Here is a sample response to question 1.

I believe that Jing-Mei's resistance to play the piano was a rebellion against her mother. Suyuan imposed piano playing on her daughter. She did not ask Jing-Mei if she wanted to play the piano. She told her to do it and expected her strict cooperation. She silenced her voice as a human being, and in so doing, made her very angry. I believe this kind of resentment stays in a child's mind for a very long time, influencing everything she does.

Suyuan also expected her daughter to be a winner, the best. Suyuan had fantasies of her daughter becoming a child prodigy, just like the one she saw on the *Ed Sullivan Show* in the fifties. In a sense, she is what could be called the worst kind of "stage mother," a mother whose sole aim in life is to get her daughter on stage and hang around behind the scenes while she performs. She hoped to find her own identity in her daughter's successes, not taking into account the daughter's feelings.

Suyuan took away her daughter's choice. Then she used exaggerated expectation to take away any pleasure Jing-Mei might have had actually playing the piano. Jing-Mei knew she could not live up to her mother's expectations, so why bother trying? She knew that trying and failing would hurt more than not trying at all. That way her mother would blame her for not trying enough; so, she skirted the whole issue by avoiding trying at all.

Mothers should listen to their daughters when they complain about one task or another. They should give their daughters choices; this way, they will develop a stronger sense of self and self-esteem. Perhaps in China Suyuan's mother's behavior would have been considered normal and acceptable. The difficulty is when these values of perfectionism for offspring are transplanted here.

The Film *The Joy Luck Club*

Characters from *The Joy Luck Club:* Suyuan Woo and Jing-Mei "June" Woo, Lindo Jong and Waverly Jong, Ying-ying St. Clair and Lena St. Clair, An-mei Hsu and Rose Hsu Jordan (*The Joy Luck Club;* dir. Wayne Wang, 1993). (Photograph courtesy of the Film Stills Archive of the Museum of Modern Art, New York.)

Optional Activities

Rent a copy of the movie *The Joy Luck Club.*

1. How is the story presented differently in the movie, *The Joy Luck Club?* Be specific as to the differences. What new perceptions did you gain about the mother/daughter relationships from the movie?
2. How do you feel the movie changed your perception about the characters Rose and Jing-Mei (June) in the book?
3. Write your response to the ending of the movie. How did you feel about it? If Amy Tan were to write a sequel to this movie, what would you like to see happen to the characters?

A dialogue from the film follows. In it, Suyuan is talking to June. June has just had a fight with Waverly, who told June that her writing had been rejected by her company. June has just told her mother that she will never be able to live up to her expectations.

Suyuan

Never expect, only hope. Hope what's best for you.

June

No? Well, it hurt. Because every time I couldn't deliver; it hurt. It hurt, Mommy. And no matter what you hope for, I'll never be more than what I am. And you never see that . . . what I really am.

Suyuan
(Taking off necklace)

Since you baby time, I wear next to my heart. It will help you to know I see you. I see you. [Referring to the dinner that they had just eaten where all the aunties and daughters and their families had gotten together.] That bad crab only you try to take. Everybody try to take best quality. They take best quality crab. You—worst. Because you have best quality heart. You have style no one can teach. . . . [you] must be born this way. I see you.

Questions about the Dialogue

Watch the whole film segment that contains the preceding dialogue and answer the questions.

1. What do you think June is saying about expectations and identity?
2. What kind of style is her mother talking about?
3. What does she mean when she says, "I see you"?
4. Compare the meaning of "I see you" with Jimmy's "I know you" in the excerpt from the script of *Mi Familia* in chapter 2.

Additional Questions for Writing and Discussion

1. In this chapter, we have discussed two of the problems immigrants experience when they come to the United States. They must deal with age differences between themselves and earlier generations, and they must deal with cultural differences between their native countries and the new one. Write an essay showing how Jing-Mei and Rose had to deal with differences between themselves and their mothers. Be as specific as possible.

2. If you were a friend or relative of their families, what advice would you have given to the mothers in the two Amy Tan excerpts? What advice would you have given the daughters?

3. Is the immigrant experience of June and Rose similar to that described by Julia Alvarez in chapter 4? Is it similar to Eva Hoffman's experience? Is there a commonality in emigrant girls across cultures or not? Explain your response.

Chapter 6
Culture, Identity, and Work

Introduction

Among the variables that can affect the ability to gain a new identity is the capacity to transfer job skills, interests, or hobbies and to continue one's line of work or profession in the new country. The role assumed on the job is often related to the public identity and incorporates use of the public language. For many working immigrants, the world of work offers another self that may incorporate aspects of both the public and private personality. This usually stable domain can represent a sort of "halfway station" into the public world.

In Chang-rae Lee's 1995 novel *Native Speaker*, the protagonist, Henry Park, makes his living as a private detective and undercover operative, a sort of real-world spy. He is adept at being a spy and assuming a third identity, partly because as a Korean American immigrant, he is used to being inconspicuous and accommodating; he is used to "blending in." Asian Americans, as a group, are often the victims of a positive stereotype, that of the "good immigrant," more intelligent than the rest and thus more likely to succeed.

Park's "blending in" is reflected in the note his Anglo wife leaves for him to read when she leaves him. It is like a poem in which she lists his characteristics.

> You are surreptitious
> B+ student of life
> μrst thing hummer of Wagner and Strauss
> illegal alien
> emotional alien
> genre bug
> Yellow peril: neo-American
> great in bed
> overrated
> poppa's boy

> sentimentalist
>
> anti-romantic
>
> ____ analyst (you fill in)
>
> stranger
>
> follower
>
> traitor
>
> spy. (1995, 5)

Henry's third identity—his assigned, secret identity, his spy role—is fake, and yet it is as complex as his "real" identities. He is quite effective at his job. When he has to see a psychiatrist under his assumed name, however, he comes dangerously close to losing his assumed identity.

> In his earnestness, Dr. Luzan kept delving further into my psyche, plumbing the depths. I was developing into a model case. Of course, I was switching between him and me, getting piecemeals of the doctor with projections in an almost classical mode, but for the first time I found myself at moments running short of my story, my chosen narrative. Normally I would have ceased matters temporarily, retreated to Westchester to reiterate and revise. But inexplicably I began stringing the legend back upon myself. I was no longer extrapolating; I was looping it through the core, freely talking about my life, suddenly breaching the confidences of my father and my mother and my wife. I even spoke to him about a lost dead son. I was becoming dangerously frank, inconsistently schizophrenic. I ceased listening to him altogether. Like a good doctor he let me go on and on, and in moments I felt he was the only one in the world who might comfort me. (1995, 22)

Besides delving into Henry Park's psychological identity as he searches for his new hybrid self, the novel *Native Speaker* in many ways is about the generation gap, and about sons and fathers, much in the way that *The Joy Luck Club* was about daughters and mothers. Just as Henry Park found himself drawn to Luzan, the psychiatrist, he is also drawn to a number of other male adult characters: his rough-hewn father; the elegant congressman Kwang, who is a kind of idealized self; and his boss, Hoagland. The novel also focuses on Park's relationship with his son Mitt; the tragic episode in which he loses him is a metaphor for losing his hybrid self. In much of the novel Park is a mystery, not only to his wife but to himself. He seems to be detached, like Eva Hoffman, but to the point of being almost invisible. His unique sort of job, that of a spy or private detective, helps him to hide.

Chang-rae Lee's *Native Speaker*

Born in Seoul, Korea, in 1965, Lee immigrated to the United States with his parents when he was three. The son of a psychiatrist, he grew up in and around New York City and graduated from Phillips Exeter Academy. After graduating from Yale in 1987, with a B.A. in English, he went on to receive a master of fine arts in creative writing from the University of Oregon. As of this writing, he is a professor at Hunter College of the City University of New York, teaching fiction writing and literature. He was recently named one of the most important new writers of the decade by the *New Yorker* magazine.

The following excerpt is from Chang-rae Lee's acclaimed novel *Native Speaker,* in which his protagonist, Henry Park, his wife, Lelia, and their son, Mitt, are described.

> Our boy, Mitt, was exactly seven years old when he died, just around the age when you really start wondering about your kid. Then, you look long at his tender arms and calves and you wish you could keep him inside the house for the next ten years, buckled up and helmeted. But all of a sudden, more than you know, he's outside somewhere, sometimes even alone, crossing the streets, scaling rocks, wrestling with dogs, swimming in pits, getting into everything mechanical and combustible and toxic. You suddenly notice that all of his friends are wild, bad kids, the kind that hold lighted firecrackers until the very last second, or torment the neighborhood animals. Mitt, the clean and bright one—somehow, miraculously, ours—runs off with them anyway, shouting the praises of his perfect life.
>
> From the time he was four we spent whole summers up at my father's house in Ardsley, mostly so Mitt could troop about on the grass and earth and bugs—the city offering only broken swings and dry swimming pools—and Lelia and I seemed to share an understanding of what would be safest and most healthful for him.
>
> My father would call me each year a few days before Memorial Day and say as if he didn't really care, *Ya, oh-noon-guh-ya?* And I would answer him and say yes, we were coming again this summer, and he could get things ready for us.

The city, of course, seemed too dangerous. Especially during the summer, the streets so dog mad with heat, untempered, literally steaming with possibilities, none of them good. People got meaner, stuck beneath all that hard light and stone. They worked through it by talking, speaking, shouting and screaming, in every language on earth. And the cursing: in New York City, summer is the season of bad language. It shouts at you from propped-up windows, it hangs on gold chains out of cars, it lingers at phone booths, peep booths, in every standing line for movies and museums and methadone.

And then there were the heat waves, the crime waves. The clouds of soot and dust. In the evenings it all descended unseen, an invisible ash of distant fires, soiling us everywhere.

So escape. Rent a car, pack it up, drive right into the heart of dreamland. Here, it went by names like Bronxville, Scarsdale, Chappaqua, Ardsley. The local all-stars.

We wanted our boy to know a cooler, softer ground. On the expansive property of my father's house stood high poplar, oak, the few elm not yet fallen with disease. They didn't appear much different to me than they did twenty years before; they looked just as tall, as venerable, the capital of my father's life. And there would wend Mitt, the child of ceaseless movement, leafy stick in hand, poking beneath the shady skirts of the trees for the smallest signs of life.

Lelia and I would watch him from the back patio. My father slept in the sun with a neon-orange golf cap pulled down over his eyes. Sometimes he spoke from beneath it, his weary Korean mumbling and I could only read the embroidery of the work *Titleist* in place of actually understanding him. Mitt would shout for us from the trees, holding up something too small to see. My father would groan in acknowledgment, lowing the refrain of my youth. *Yahhh*. Mitt unconcerned, hopped a little dance, his patented jig, waving madly, legs pumping. We waved back. I shouted to him, too loud.

He brought back rocks to us. Dead insects. Live slugs, green pennies, bits of faded magazines. Every kind and condition of bark. Stuff, he said. He arranged them carefully next to my father's chaise like trinkets for barter, all the while recounting to himself in a small voice the catalogue of his suburban treasure. He offered the entire lot to my father.

"I give you a dollar," my father said to the man.

"Two!" Mitt cried.

"Lucky silver dollar," the old man countered, as if luck had meant anything in his life.

"The one on your desk?"

"You go get it now," he said, pointing up to the top window of the house.

Mitt liked to carry the coin with him. I knew because he would produce it wherever we were and start rubbing the face with his thumb. My father must have advised him so, told him some Bronze Age Korean mythology to go with it, the tale of a lost young prince whose magic coin is sole proof of his rightful seat and destiny.

A week after the accident, when the nurse at the hospital desk gave me the plastic bag of his clothes, I found the coin in the back flap pocket of his shorts. The coin was warm—the bag must have been left near a window—and I wondered how long the shiny metal could hold in a heat, if it could remember something like the press of flesh.

He loved the old man, adored him. Whenever you looked, Mitt was scaling the wide bow of that paternal back, or swinging from his shoulders, or standing on the tops of his feet so that they walked in tandem, with ponderous, doubled soles.

There were certain concordances. In profile, you saw the same blunt line descend the back of their necks, those high, flat ears, but then little else because Lelia—or maybe her father—had endowed Mitt with that other, potent sprawl of limbs, those round, vigilant eyes, the upturned ancestral nose (like a scrivener's, in my imagination), his boy's form already so beautifully jumbled and subversive and historic. No one, I thought, had ever looked like that.

The kids in my father's neighborhood gave him trouble that first summer. One afternoon Mitt tugged at my pant leg and called me innocently, in succession, a *chink*, a *jap*, a *gook*. I couldn't immediately respond and so he said them again, this time adding, in singsong, "Charlie Chan, face as flat as a frying pan."

They're just words, I then told him firmly, confidently—in the way a father believes he should—but mostly because I didn't know what else to say. And after the same kids saw Lelia and me play with him in the front yard they started in with other things, teaching him words like mutt, mongrel, half-breed, banana, twinkie. One day Mitt came home with his clothes soiled and said that they had pushed him down to the ground and put dirt in his mouth. He proudly told my father that he hadn't cried. Lelia, who up to now had been liberal and assured, started shrieking angrily about suburbia, America, the brand of culture we had to live in, and packed Mitt up the stairs to scrub his muddy face, telling him all the while how wonderful he was.

That evening my father and I went around the neighborhood to talk to the parents. We walked stiffly in silence on those manicured streets, and it seemed a repetition of a moment from many years before, when an older boy named Clay had taken away my cap pistol. I remembered how my father had spoken to Clay's mother in a halting, polite English and how he had excused her son for taking advantage of my timidity and misunderstandings.

"My son," he explained, "is no good for friends." The woman hardly understood what he said, and Clay—grinning to himself behind her and looking more menacing than ever—only temporarily handed over my toy gun.

Now, as the first front door opened, I spoke calmly and severely, explaining the situation as one of gravity but not crisis. But then, at the sight of the offending boy, the old man behind me inexplicably exploded, chopping the air with his worn fingers, cursing red-faced like a cheated peasant in our throaty mother tongue until the bewildered child began to cry. His mother protested meekly (you could tell she knew my father) and I, too, wanted him to stop yelling, to shut up and let me speak. Instead I allowed myself to sacrifice this boy and his mother, perhaps even myself, and let the old man yell this one bloody murder, if only for Mitt.

I know this: a child doesn't forgive or forget—he works it out.

By that last summer Mitt was thick with them all. Friends for life, or so it must have seemed. I knew their names once, could place them with their well-fed faces. After he died they all seemed to get hidden away somewhere, like sets of precious china, and eventually I forgot everything about them.

But for a long time the little arms and legs and voices were part of my nightly ritual before sleep. Like a cinematic mantra, a mystical trailer of memory, I replayed the scene of all those boys standing in the grass about the spontaneous crèche of his death. Lelia knew I did this with the night, she would grasp my hand until she couldn't wait any longer for me to say something, and finally she would fall asleep. When her hand went limp, I would let myself wander over the ground of what happened. I could only see it when she slumbered. I needed her right next to me, I thought, bodied up, but off in another world.

I was just coming back from the store with more soda and candy for the birthday party. A boy came running out toward the car, leaping and waving his hands, he was sick-looking, half-smiling and jumping. As I turned the car into the driveway I heard nervous, confused shouts echoing from the backyard through the tops of the trees. I ran around the side of the house without turning off the ignition. All the boys were standing there lock-kneed. In the middle of them was Lelia, sitting on the grass, cradling his dead blue head in her arms and lap and rocking on her knees. She was wailing nothing I could understand or remember now, and she sounded like someone else, an anybody on the street. A boy to my side was crying fitfully and telling me between gasps how they didn't mean to stay on him as long as they did. *It was just a big stupid dog pile,* he kept shouting, *it was just a big stupid dog pile.* And then my father came out from the sliding porch door and saw me, a cordless phone in his hand, and he yelled in Korean that the ambulance was coming. But before he made it to us his legs seemed to fold under him and he sat back unnaturally on the matted lawn, his face so small-looking, arrested, so short of breath.

I bent down and started blowing into Mitt's mouth. Lelia cried that she'd tried already. She kept screaming about it and I had to tell her to shut up. I didn't know what I was doing. I pulled open his mouth and blew anyway, a dozen times, a hundred, pumping down on his chest with all my weight, eventually pounding on him as if he were solid ground. I shudder to think that I might have injured him, hurt his delicate breastbone or his ribs, or worse, that his last thought was to ask why his father was harming him. I've read the dying feel no pain but sense everything that goes on around them. They view the scene from a brief distance above and no matter who they are or how old, they gain a wisdom from that last vista. But we are the living, remaining on the ground, and what we know is the narrow and the broken. Here, we are strewn about in the lengthy expanse of an archipelago, too far to call one another, too far to see.

During certain nights, I pulled a half-sleeping Lelia back onto my body, right onto my chest, and breathed as barely as I could without falling faint. She let herself balance on me until she was no longer touching the bed. She knew what to do, what to do to me, that I was Mitt, that then she was Mitt, our pile of two as heavy as the balance of all those boys who had now grown up. We nearly pressed each other to death, our swollen lips and eyes wishing upon ourselves the fall of tears, that great free anger, that great obese heft of melancholy, enough of it piling on at once so that sometimes whether we wanted to or not we made love so hard and gritty we had to say fuck to be telling the very first part of the truth. In the bed, in the space between us, it was about the sad way of all flesh, alive or dead or caught in between, it was about what must happen between people who lose forever the truest moment of their union. Flesh, the pressure, the rhymes of gasps. This was all we could find in each other, this the novel language of our life.

Morning brought sober hope, then the usual imperatives. Look for Lelia (she was most often gone before I woke, already off somewhere in the city working with students). Now, keep thinking. Think for keeps. Then, isolate the wonderments, the curiosities of his death; they will help you to see. Shed sentimentality. Stop this falling in love with fate. Reside, if you can, in the last place of the dead.

Maybe this way:

A crush. You pale little boys are crushing him, your adoring mob of hands and feet, your necks and heads, your nostrils and knees, your still-sweet sweat and teeth and grunts. Too thick anyway, to breathe. How pale his face, his chest. Blanket his eyes. Listen, now you can hear the attempt of his breath, that unlost voice, calling us from the bottom of the world. (1995, 100–107)

Questions for Writing and Discussion

1. Do you think that all children call newcomers by nicknames? If they do, at what age might they stop?
2. Do you think that Mitt's death could have been avoided? Explain. Do you think that racism played a part?
3. How did the parents try to console themselves after the boy died?
4. Park says that he felt that the dead gain a "wisdom from that last vista," the scene where the living are saying good-bye. Why do you think he felt that way?
5. Do you think that Mitt, who is half Asian and half Caucasian, could be considered a metaphor in the novel? Why or why not?

Student Writing Sample

Here is a sample response to question 2.

> The episode where Mitt gets killed left me saddened and confused. His racial stereotyping and racism cause the children to play so roughly that they crushed the little boy?
>
> It is amazing that children that young could be so mean. Where were his parents? They must have trusted the neighborhood and its children. If they knew that the kids in the neighborhood at Ardsley were bad, why did they not monitor their play?
>
> Ironic that the accident happened in the suburbs when the family wanted to get away from the city to be in a safer, healthier environment for the boy.
>
> The relationship between his grandfather and the little boy was touching, and unexpected when you think that the boy was half white. The grandfather represented the old way of life, telling him myths about coins. The interchange between Mitt's family and one of the moms in the neighborhood was very telling and foreshadowed the tragedy.
>
> I wonder if this fictional account of childhood cruelty is based on a real incident or not. The grief the parents felt and their attempts to cope were very realistic. I wonder if their marriage will last?

What's in a Name?

You may have noticed that Korean American students, as well as other Asian students, adopt American names that they use in school and in the public culture, instead of their native Korean names. I once asked a friend why this is so, and she told me that Koreans as a group have tended to recognize that Americans would find their names hard to pronounce, and rather than hear their names constantly mispronounced, they would rather change them to American or public names. (The Korean name would still be used at home.)

An essay by Chang-rae Lee about changing his name follows. This essay originally appeared on a website of the Putnam Berkeley Group in 1995–96.

> One day my mother asked me if I was ready to choose a name.
> I was five years old. Of course I already had a name, the one I have now, but even then I knew what she meant. In the coming fall I would enter the first grade of elementary school, the first year of my formal

schooling, and my mother, heeding the suggestions of the kindergarten teacher and school counselor, was determined to give me every aid and advantage.

First, he must learn English, at all costs he must learn English, and with a good accent. So in my room I found piles of books, and I could watch as much television as I wished, and she and my father would speak to me only in Korean, to protect my impressionable ears.

Next, the boy would need an American name. This was more difficult for her, because all those funny-sounding names held no meaning for her, no nuance or significance. An old astrologer who consulted ancient charts and equations had chosen my Korean name, matching the exact time of my birth on this day, of this month, of that Year of the Snake, with certain characters, to arrive at the most auspicious of combinations.

But here in America she had to leave the crucial naming to me. So I looked to my books, to the newspapers, and then to the television, and for weeks I couldn't decide between Greg and Peter and Bobby. But Greg and Peter and Bobby really weren't like me, they lived in a giant house and with a maid, and thought they had troubles—theirs weren't anything like mine.

My friends in the apartment building were no more of a help. They gave me names that they considered neat or cool, names they wished one of their friends to have: Buzz, Rocky, Speed. One kid, not quite getting it, suggested the name *Tom Seaver* (*the year was 1970*).

My father had his own ideas. He didn't seem terribly concerned either way, but he thought that if it had to be, I should sport something respectable, intelligent, like William or Walter. But those names seemed too old. And his bookshelves of psychology—Sigmund, Alfred, Erich, Rollo—led me nowhere.

Finally, I settled on solid middle ground, names I was sure were 100% American, unremarkable, easy to say, and most important, normal: Chris, David, Mike, James, Ray, and then the one I came closest to being, Chuck. Of all things—Chuck. I would write *Lee* after all of them, scribe them out at the top of separate pages, to see how they looked, worked. I had my friends call me Ray for a week, Chuck for another, but they would always forget, and so would I; I'd acknowledge them when they called my Korean name. I'd forget the whole day the person I was trying to be.

I was trying so hard to make it easier for them, and for strangers, the idea being that if we make it simpler for them it would be simpler and easier for me. No more fumbling of my name on the first day of class, no more taunts of "Chang-a chink-a" in the playground, no more questions of what I was, or where I came from, no more of that constant trouble and confusion.

But even the alias *Chuck* didn't help. Maybe the name made me a little bit more American in those others' eyes, but not enough to make a real difference. The project slowly faded. I went back to writing out my own name, practicing it, as if in reacquaintance. And somewhere inside, I was just beginning to understand that who I was couldn't change at all, ever, that I couldn't dress up in another boy's clothes. I wasn't being smart or proud. I would stare into the mirror and try my best. But simply nothing fit. And if Chuck or Ray couldn't run or play any easier in the world, then it would have to be just me, out there, old name and all. (1995, 1–2)

Acculturation and Identity through Work or Hobby

In *Native Speaker*, the protagonist, Henry Park, was very adept at being a spy. Being good at something always helps adjustment. Sometimes, a newly arrived student will find it easier to adapt to a new culture if there is a part-time job, hobby, or talent at which he or she excels. As an expression of self, a hobby or talent can give positive feedback. Nieto corroborates this idea in the case study of a successful African American student, Rich Miller, who has developed a tremendous amount of independence and pride. Music occupies a central part of the young man's life, as he explains in the following excerpt.

> I plan on keeping my music up. I really don't have hobbies and I don't play too many sports or anything like this, so I really think this keeps me going. It gives me something to go for from day to day. And you learn something new all the time. (1996, 61)

If Eva Hoffman and June in the *Joy Luck Club* had found the right kind of encouragement to develop prodigious talent at the piano, it might have been easier for them to have found an identity as a child and a niche among fellow musicians.

Stereotyping Asian Students: High Expectations

In a case study of Hoang Vinh, a Southest Asian immigrant, Nieto discusses the high expectations that most Asian children perceive in U.S. culture. During interviews with Hoang Vinh, Nieto found that for many Southeast Asian students, a high standard exists with regard to being "educated," including being able to get along with people. Vinh explained this as "wanting to know about other people and about the world and wanting to be able to get along with and help others." By "educated people," he refers not only to academics but also to behaviors not always related to studies. Grades are not as important as being the best you can (1996, 180).

An essay from *Newsweek* about Asian American children follows. It was written by Ted Gup, a Fulbright scholar to China.

Who Is a Whiz Kid?
Because my sons are Asian-American, people jump to conclusions about their academic gifts.

Shortly after joining a national magazine some years ago as a writer, I found myself watching in horror as the week's cover story was prepared. The story was about "Asian-American whiz kids," and it featured a series of six student portraits, each face radiating with an intellectual brilliance. Being new to the enterprise, I was at first tentative in my criticism, cautioning that such a story was inherently biased and fueled racial and ethnic stereotypes. My criticism was dismissed. "This is something good we are saying about them," one top editor remarked. I reduced my criticism to writing. "What," I asked, "would be the response if the cover were about 'Jewish whiz kids'? Would anyone really dare to produce such an obviously offensive story?" My memo was ignored. Not long after, the cover appeared on the nation's newsstands, and the criticism began to fly. The editors were taken aback.

As a former Fulbright scholar to China I have long taken a strong interest in the portrayal of Asian-Americans. But my interest went well beyond the academic. Even as the cover was being prepared, I was waiting to adopt my first son from Korea. His name was to be David. He was 5 months old when he arrived. That did not stop even some otherwise sophisticated friends from volunteering that he would no doubt be a good student. Probably a mathematician, they opined, with a tone that uncomfortably straddled jest and prediction. I tried to take it all with good humor, this idea that a 5-month-old who could not yet sit up, speak a word or control his bowels was already destined for academic greatness. Even his major seemed foreordained.

Many Asian-Americans seem to walk an uneasy line between taking pride in their remarkable achievements and needing to shake off stereotypes. The jokes abound. There is the apocryphal parent who asks, "Where is the other point?" when his or her child scores a 99 on a test. Another familiar refrain has the young Asian-American student enumerating his or her hobbies: "studying, studying and more studying."

Several months after David arrived he and I entered a small mom-and-pop convenience store in our neighborhood. The owners were Korean. I noticed that the husband, standing behind the cash register, was eyeing my son. "Is he Korean?" he asked. "Yes," I nodded. He reached out for him and took him in his arms. "He'll be good in math," declared the man. "My god," I muttered. Not him, too!

It was preposterous. It was funny. And it was unnerving. Embedded in such elevated expectations were really threats to my son. Suppose, I wondered, he should turn out to be only a mediocre student, or worse yet, not a student at all. I resented the stereotypes and saw them for what they were, the other side of the coin of racism. It is easy to delude one's self into thinking it harmless to offer racial compliments, but that is an inherent contradiction in terms. Such sweeping descriptives, be they negative or positive, deny the other thing most precious to all peoples—individuality. These stereotypes are pernicious for two reasons. First, such attributes are relative and tend to pit one race against another. Witness the seething enmity in many inner cities between Korean store owners and their African-American patrons. Stereotypes that hint at superiority in one race implicitly suggest inferiority in another. They are ultimately divisive, and in their most virulent form, even deadly. Who can forget the costs of the Aryan myth?

Such stereotypes also place a crushing burden on Asian-Americans. Few would deny that disproportionate numbers of Asian surnames appear each year among the winners of the Westinghouse science prizes or in the ranks of National Merit Scholars. But it might be a reflection of parental influences, personal commitment and cultural predilections, not genetic predisposition. A decade ago, as a Fulbright Lecturer in Beijing, I saw my Chinese students devoted to their studies. Were my students in the United States to invest similar time in their books I would have every reason to expect similar results.

I have often been told that Koreans are the "Jews of Asia," a reference to both their reported skills in business and their inherent intelligence. As a Jew, I cannot help but wince at such descriptions. I remember being one of the very few of my faith in a Midwest boarding school. There were many presumptions weighing on me, most of them grounded in my religion. My own classroom performance almost singlehandedly disabused my teachers of the myth that Jews were academically gifted. I barely made it through. Whether it was a lack of intelligence or simple rebellion against expectation, I do not know. I do know that more than once the fact that I was Jewish was raised as evidence that I could and should be doing better. Expectations based on race, be they raised or lowered, are no less galling.

David is now in the first grade. He is already taking math with the second graders and asking me about square roots and percentiles. I think back to the Korean merchant who took him in his arms and pronounced him a math whiz. Was he right? Do Asian-Americans have it easier, endowed with some special strand of DNA? The answer is a resounding no. Especially in our house. My son David has learning disabilities to overcome and what progress he has made is individual in the purest and most heroic sense. No one can or should take that away from him, suggesting he is just another wunderkind belonging to a favored race.

A year after my first son arrived, we adopted his brother from Korea. His name is Matthew. Let it be known that Matthew couldn't care less about math. He's a bug man. Slugs and earthworms. I suspect he will never be featured on any cover stories about Asian-American whiz kids, but I will continue to resist anything and anyone who attempts to dictate either his interests or his abilities based on race or place of birth. Bugs are fine by me and should be more than fine by him. (1997, 21)

Questions for Writing and Discussion

1. Do you agree with author Gup's opinion about stereotyping of Asian children? Is this bad or good for the child?
2. Can you see potential conflicts in a multicultural classroom because of stereotyping?

What Is Education?

Just as cultural ideals toward education vary from culture to culture, the same is true of what is considered good writing. For example, good writing in Spanish includes digression and formal repetition, which can be a stylistic variation that dates back to the oral tradition of Latin witnesses (Santana-Seda 1975).

Research by Li (1996) found that good writing in Chinese is not so much the ability to defend a point using specifics as it is the ability to poetically express ideas. The more closely ideas can serve society, the better the writing is considered.

In contrast, in the United States the writing has to express the writer's sentiments as authentically as possible. Li concludes her study by making the point that as standards for good writing vary from culture to culture, writing teachers should acquaint themselves with the students' native cultures and styles of writing. The same can be said for education in other fields.

The idea of education means different things in different cultural contexts. In Latin cultures, a person is considered educated if he or she is well behaved. It can sometimes be difficult to get students from these cultures to learn to communicate directly and assertively. This can affect various tasks in the classroom in which students have to use initiative, including problem-posing, problem-solving in discussions, and forming a thesis (or argument) for expository writing.

Questions for Writing and Discussion

1. Write a broad definition for the word *education.* Then look up the word in the dictionary and find the Latin derivative. How and why do you think the word is often misused and misinterpreted?
2. Stereotyping, or overgeneralizing, can be positive as well as negative. Give several examples of positive stereotypes of different ethnic groups.
3. How can teachers help dispel stereotypes?
4. Can you think of many variations in educational systems that exist here in the United States?
5. How do you think education differs within different cultures?

The Asian Stereotype: Model Americans

Though each immigrant group has a great deal in common with other immigrant groups, there are differences as well. In an article, "Voices of Korean American Women," Eda Harris-Hastick, a professor at City University of New York, says "Another myth used to describe Asian Americans is the common misperception that Asian Americans are quiet, hardworking immigrants, who are presumably 'making it' in American society." This myth, known as the "model minority" myth, is a social construction that first surfaced in the 1960s at a time when the United States was experiencing political, economic, and social turmoil (Harris-Hastick, 1996). This stereotype—often considered a positive one—was used as a means of showcasing Asians as a model minority, as an unassuming, nonrioting, nonrebelling group whose members were quietly succeeding through hard work at a time when African Americans were angrily and noisily demanding help from the federal government through federally supported social programs. The so-called model minority accounts praised Asian Americans as "extraordinary" immigrant families and gave accolades to their children, who were excelling academically, especially in math and science. The myth attempted to label Asian Americans and set them apart from other immigrant groups as hardworking self-sufficient, self-reliant immigrants (Harris-Hastick 1996). By comparison, other immigrant groups whose talents lay in different areas of life, say, sports or music, could be discredited as "lazy."

Questions for Writing and Discussion

Can you think of other immigrant groups that have been troubled by stereotyping, both negative and positive? How can we help prevent thinking in stereotypes?

Chapter 7
Identity, Class, and Race

Introduction

This chapter will focus on two very complex issues, race and class. Because of the complexity of these issues, it's not possible to explore them completely here. We can however focus on the issues that relate to identity and African American culture.

The Legacy of Slavery

As we have seen, one of the things that can make an immigrant's transition more difficult is if the immigrant has not come by his or her own choice. In chapters 3 and 4, we discussed how difficult it is for children or adolescents such as Eva Hoffman and Julia Alvarez, who were brought to a new country by their parents and had no choice in where they would live. A much greater problem, as is obvious, is the case of those who were brought here as slaves.

Here is an account of cruelty toward slaves drawn from *Incidents in the Life of a Slave Girl*, the first slave narrative written by a woman in the United States. Harriet Jacobs, who wrote under the pseudonym Linda Brent, lived from 1813 to 1897. Her account was first published in 1861.

> Cruelty is contagious in uncivilized communities. Mr. Conant, a neighbor of Mr. Litch, returned from town one evening in a partial state of intoxication. His body servant gave him some offence. He was divested of his clothes, except his shirt, whipped, and tied to a large tree in front of the house. It was a stormy night in winter. The wind blew bitterly cold, and the boughs of the old tree crackled under falling sleet. A member of the family, fearing he would freeze to death, begged that he might be taken down; but the master would not relent. He remained there three hours; and, when he was cut down, he was more dead than alive. (Brent 1973, 47)

Underlying the atrocity of slavery are the racist or prejudiced beliefs about those enslaved. These beliefs were used to justify the right to own slaves in the United States. African Americans suffered as slaves throughout the first half of this country's history, and the racism and elitism that enabled slavery to exist, including the feeling of entitlement referred to as "white privilege," have continued to plague subsequent generations.

Furthermore, African Americans are the targets of the projections of society's negative emotions, scapegoats for the Anglo culture's disappointments. Thus, the dominant Anglo culture has attempted to brainwash all Americans, particularly African Americans, to believe in a negative stereotype of racial inferiority. For more than one hundred years after emancipation, little esteem was granted to the African American culture.

Questions for Writing and Discussion

1. Have you ever been or do you know anyone who has been the subject of racism? Explain.
2. Have you ever observed "white privilege"? Can you give examples of white privilege?
3. Do you think that racism will be solved in the new millennium, or will it remain a cause of violence, tragedy, and unhappiness? Why?

Zora Neale Hurston

Early in the twentieth century, African American writer Zora Neale Hurston explored issues of race, culture, class, and identity in powerful ways. Though she did not use her writing as a polemic against racism, the exploration of her native Florida's African American population is appreciated as a celebration of its culture, much of which can be traced back to Africa.

Hurston was born in Eatonville, a poor, all-black town in Florida. Her father was a minister, and she lost her mother at an early age. For years she wandered around the country with a theater group. In the 1920s she wound up in New York at the height of the Harlem renaissance. A brilliant student, she studied anthropology at Columbia with the famed Franz Boas, through whom she became interested in studying and writing about the folklore of her native Florida. She received a federal grant that gave her the funds to work in the "field." She also studied "hoodoo" in New Orleans and in Jamaica.

Hurston's writing was not well received by her contemporaries. Her authentic way of rendering black culture and dialogue was severely criticized and considered offensive or demeaning by some, including Richard Wright and other renowned black authors. Although she was quite prolific, her work was largely overlooked until after her death.

Recently her body of work was rediscovered by Alice Walker and Maya Angelou. Now she is not only appreciated for her record of her people's folklore but for its authentic celebration of a culture. Furthermore, as someone who was raised poor and who became a scholar, an anthropologist, and a writer, she is an important role model for African American women (Hemenway 1977).

A Controversial Figure

Even today, Zora Neale Hurston is at the center of much controversy. The issues that surround the controversy can be summarized in two main ideas.

First, Hurston's use of indigenous language from the rural community of her native Florida is sometimes interpreted as portraying black people there as "quaint and uneducated." However, when her writing is examined in the light of her avocation as an ethnographer who recorded rural black dialect and folklore dispassionately and accurately, this claim makes no sense. As an anthropologist, she knew how to detach herself and attain an insider-outsider point of view. She did not feel that she had to pander to any authority or particular audience. She wanted to tell the truth as she saw it; she studied a culture that had never been examined before and portrayed that culture in her writing with respect and vivacious humor (Bloom 1986, 35).

Second, Zora Neale Hurston did not use her work and her writing as a platform to fight racism. For this she is criticized. Hurston was proud of her race, however, and pitied "white folks" because she felt they had no soul or light. She also spoke about the unfairness of racism in her writing. One example among many is her essay "What White People Won't Publish" (Hurston 1979, 67–73), in which she faults white publishers for wanting to print only material that stereotyped minorities. Hurston's gift to her people was in her own strength and self-awareness. Her health with regard to race is evident; she was completely herself and asked to be validated not just as a member of a group but on her own merit, as a creative and unique genius and as a human being (Walker in Hurston 1979, 5).

In the following excerpt from *Dust Tracks on a Road*, Hurston's autobiography, she explores the topic of racial perceptions. In it you will encounter her unique take on the topics of racial identity, solidarity, stereotypes, and class-based prejudice. As you read, remember Hurston's perspective as an anthropologist and her love of her people's folktales. She entitled the chapter "My People! My People!"

"My people! My people!" From the earliest rocking of my cradle days, I have heard this cry go up from Negro lips. It is forced outward by pity, scorn and hopeless resignation. It is called forth by the observations of one class of Negro on the doings of another branch of the brother in black. For instance, well-mannered Negroes groan out like that when they board a train or a bus and find other Negroes on there with their shoes off, stuffing themselves with fried fish, bananas and peanuts, and throwing the garbage on the floor. Maybe they are not only eating and drinking. The offenders may be "loud-talking" the place, and holding back nothing of their private lives, in a voice that embraces the entire coach. The well-dressed Negro shrinks back in his seat at that, shakes his head and sighs, "My people!"

Now, the well-mannered Negro is embarrassed by the crude behavior of the others. They are not friends, and have never seen each other before. So why should he or she be embarrassed? It is like this: The well-bred Negro has looked around and seen America with his eyes. He or she has set himself to measure up to what he thinks of as the white standard of living. He is conscious of the fact that the Negro in America needs more respect if he expects to get any acceptance at all. Therefore, after straining nerve to get an education, maintain an attractive home, dress decently, and otherwise conform, he is dismayed at the sight of other Negroes tearing down what he is trying to build up. It is every day, "And that good-for-nothing, trashy Negro is the one the white people judge us all by. They think we're all just alike. My people! My people!"

So the quiet-spoken Negro man or woman who finds himself in the midst of one of these "broadcasts" as on the train, cannot go over and say "Don't act like that, brother. You're giving us all a black eye." He or she would know better than to try that. The performance would not only go on, it would get better with the "dickty" Negro as the butt of all the quips. The educated Negro may know all about the differential calculus and the theory of evolution, but he is fighting entirely out of his class when he tries to quip with the underprivileged. The bookless may have difficulty in reading a paragraph in a newspaper, but when they get down to "playing the dozens" they have no equal in America, and I'd risk a sizeable bet, in the whole world. Starting off in first by calling you a seven-sided son-of-a-bitch, and pausing to name the sides, they proceed to "specify" until the tip-top branch of your family tree has been "given a reading." No profit in that to the upper class Negro, so he minds his own business and groans, "My people! My people!"

It being a traditional cry, I was bound to hear it often and under many circumstances. But it is not the only folk label that I heard. "Race Pride"—"Race Prejudice"—"Race Man"—"Race Solidarity"—"Race Consciousness"—"Race."

"Race Prejudice" I was instructed was something bad that white people used on us. It seemed that white people felt superior to black ones and would not give Negroes justice for that reason. "Race Pride" was something that, if we had it, we would feel ourselves superior to the whites. A black skin was the greatest honor that could be blessed on any man. A "Race Man" was somebody who always kept the glory and honor of his race before him. Must stand ever ready to defend the Negro race from all hurt, harm and danger. Especially if a white person said "Nigger," "You people," "Negress" or "Darkies." It was the mark of shame if somebody accused: "Why, you are not a Race Man (or woman)." People made whole careers of being "Race" men and women. They were champions of the race. "Race Consciousness" is a plea to Negroes to bear their color in mind at all times. It was just a phrase to me when I was a child. I knew it was supposed to mean something deep. By the time I got grown I saw that it was only an imposing line of syllables, for no Negro in America is apt to forget his race. "Race Solidarity" looked like something solid in my childhood, but like all other mirages, it faded as I came close enough to look. As soon as I could think, I saw that there is no such thing as Race Solidarity in America with any group. It is freely admitted that it does not exist among Negroes. Our so-called Race Leaders cry over it. Others accept it as a natural thing that Negroes should not remain an unmelting black knot in the body politic. Our interests are too varied. Personal benefits run counter to race lines too often for it to hold. If it did, we could never fit into the national pattern. Since the race line has never held any other group in America, why expect it to be effective with us? The upper class Negroes admit it in their own phrases. The lower class Negroes say it with a tale. ([1942] 1995, 177–79)

Questions for Writing and Discussion

1. Explain what Hurston means when she says, "My People! My People!"

2. What do you think the author means when she writes, "There is no such thing as Race Solidarity in America with any group"? Hurston wrote these words in the 1930s. How does this apply to groups within today's society?

3. As an anthropologist who studied the folklore, customs, and language of African American people from her native Florida, Hurston uses these cultural phenomena when she writes. Give examples from this excerpt.

4. Summarize her basic ideas regarding stereotypes. According to Hurston, does class exist in the African American community?

5. Hurston's writing created controversy and at times was unpopular, most notably with Richard Wright, a contemporary, who claimed she had "sold out" and needed to be "more political" in her writing. Yet others claim she is a role model for African Americans, particularly women. Based on the excerpt we just read, form groups and argue a position, pro or con, regarding Hurston's position on the topics summarized in question 4.

6. An author we studied in chapter 1, Richard Rodriquez, is also a controversial figure among his people. Other Latinos have claimed that his stand on bilingual education is a betrayal. Rodriquez's position basically is that one must love a sense of private individuality (the Spanish self) in order to attain public individuality. He feels that only by being recognized first and foremost as an American can a person gain complete equality of opportunity and rights, and he celebrated the day he became Richard and not Ricardo Rodriquez (1983, 6, 7). What is your opinion of his point of view? Compare his perspective with Hurston's. Explain your response by referring to examples in the respective texts, Rodriquez's and Hurston's.

7. Besides the United States, other countries have class distinctions in their societies. What classes exist in other societies that you are aware of? How can we help our students become conscious of negative class stereotypes and elitist perception?

In the preceding excerpt we focused on Hurston's perception of class in her own race. The following excerpt, called "How It Feels to Be Colored Me," further explores Zora Neale Hurston's sense of identity with regard to the individual. It is from Hurston's collection of stories edited by Alice Walker, with the long title *I Love Myself When I Am Laughing and Then Again When I Am Looking Mean and Impressive.* Compare it to the first selection in style and tone. What can we learn about identity and race from this essay?

But I am not tragically colored. There is no great sorrow dammed up in my soul, nor lurking behind my eyes. I do not mind at all. I do not belong to the sobbing school of Negrohood who hold that nature somehow has given them a lowdown dirty deal and whose feelings are all hurt about it. Even in the helter-skelter skirmish that is my life, I have seen that the world is to the strong regardless of a little pigmentation more or less. No, I do not weep at the world—I am too busy sharpening my oyster knife.

Someone is always at my elbow reminding me that I am the granddaughter of slaves. It fails to register depression with me. Slavery is sixty years in the past. The operation was successful and the patient is doing well, thank you. The terrible struggle that made an American out of a potential slave said "On the line!" The Reconstruction said "Get set!"; and the generation before said "Go!" I am off to a flying start and I must not halt in the stretch to look behind and weep. Slavery is a price I paid for civilization, and the choice was not with me. It is a bully adventure and worth all that I have paid through my ancestors for it. No one on earth ever had a greater chance for glory. The world to be won and nothing to be lost. It is thrilling to think—to know that for any act of mine, I shall get twice as much praise or twice as much blame. It is quite exciting to hold the center of the national stage, with the spectators not knowing whether to laugh or to weep.

Questions for Writing and Discussion

1. What do you think the author means when she says, "I am not tragically colored"?
2. Explain what you think Hurston means by "No, I do not weep at the world—I am too busy sharpening my oyster knife."

3. Hurston is known for her wit and her sense of humor expressed in her writing. Can you find any expressions that show this?

4. What is meant when she writes, referring to herself, "No one on earth ever had a better chance for glory." Can you see how this could be a controversial point of view?

5. What has this essay added to what we know of Hurston's position on identity in the preceding excerpt from "My People, My People"?

Student Writing Sample

Here is a sample response to question 3.

> I think there is some similarity with regard to self-concept to Rodriguez. I believe that, like Rodriguez, Hurston wanted her private and public self to be blended. That is why she did not mind using the vernacular, then code switching to Standard English. At the same time, she differs from Richard in that she seems to be completely at home with who she is, whereas I can understand why Richard Rodriguez never seems totally comfortable.
>
> On the other hand, we are all a part of the group we belong to and Hurston seemed to want to be acknowledged more as an individual than as part of a group. Our group membership shapes who we are and helps define us. Being an anthropologist is great, but she should have been more involved with helping the cause of African Americans in her personal life. I can understand why some people are disappointed in her lack of loyalty to her race to fight discrimination.
>
> At the same time, I find her a fascinating person. I am glad to learn of her and look forward to reading more of her books.

Optional Activities

Read *Their Eyes Were Watching God*, a novel by Zora Neale Hurston, and look for more examples of metaphors that can be found throughout Hurston's books. Hurston called them "signifying speech." Can you explain why? Here is an example of one such metaphor when the protagonist describes her broken marriage: "She stood there until something fell off the shelf inside her. Then she went inside there to see what it was. It was her image of Jody tumbled down and shattered but looking at it she saw that it never was the flesh and blood figure of her dreams. Just something she had grabbed up to drape her dreams over" (1937, 82).

May Stawsky

Zora Neale Hurston wrote about the African American community in the 1930s and 1940s. We now will explore a contemporary view. The following essay offers a different perspective from that of Zora Neale Hurston. It was written in 1999 by May Stawsky, a poet and retired New York City schoolteacher, who offers a personal point of view on her identity and her family's history.

About 1840, four runaway slaves came by way of the Underground Railroad to Haddonfield, New Jersey. In Haddonfield they were aided by Quakers to reach Free Haven, a small colored settlement, later known as Snow Hill, now known as Lawnside. These slaves, Davie, Isaac, James and Hannah, abandoned their slave name and took the free name of Arthur. Their parents were dead, so the three brothers and their sister desired to remain near one another in their start of a new life. I try to read the lives between the lines describing The Arthur Family Tree. I try to imagine the scenes of danger and fear that surely must have haunted that brave foursome for the rest of their lives. Davie Arthur, the oldest, the story continues, marries and has two children, the older a girl he names Hannah after his sister. Hannah's marriage to Theodore Williams produces a daughter, Rebecca, and a son, Henry, who quite a bit later in his life is referred to by his neighbors as that "uppity Hen Williams," according to his youngest daughter, who was my mother.

The stories my mother told about her childhood in Lawnside painted a vibrant picture of a robust community struggling together, farming the land, caring for one another, learning sacrifice, discipline, and the value of humor and prayer. She felt a deep pride in the achievements of her humble hometown. I am the city kid who visited Lawnside in the summers and fell in love with the wide fields, dirt roads, farm life, and a town brimming over with uncles, aunts, and cousins. Over the years my mother's Lawnside became a mine, a cherished symbol of our history and heritage. The idea of Lawnside—a community that is a family, working together, sacrificing together, for the benefit of all—became a building block in my personal philosophy. The former "station on the Underground Railroad" surviving and enduring as a thriving town, continuing today, has become for me a testimony to what human beings can achieve together, for each other. I think of my forebears' accomplishment as the result of a sacred unity.

I was born in Harlem; played potsie on its sidewalks, darted through icy hydrant water on its streets in summer, and bundled up inside its railroad apartments when the snows came. I attended its public schools, and wore around my neck on a string the ubiquitous symbol of children whose parents went to work daily: the door key. Harlem was one of the northern centers that black families and individuals migrated to from many of the southern states in the '20s and the '30s, seeking jobs, education, and an absence of racial violence. Blacks from the West Indies, and the Hispanics of African descent, as well as a few Asian families, added to the variation in the community. With its struggling immigrant families giving encouragement and support to each other the Harlem of my youth was in many important ways an urbanized version of Lawnside. The hostile surrounding city pushed us closer together. Beyond the confines of the community, in other areas of the city, housing and job discrimination was rampant; even within the Harlem boundaries subtle color discrimination existed in housing, and white merchants on 125th Street refused to hire blacks. Many of the adults worked at service jobs in other parts of the city, and it was the children's job to study and do well in school.—Often led by the Church, families "looked out" for each other's children, organized against restricted housing, inferior schools, and job discrimination. Rituals of music and dance, literature and poetry, painting and sculpture became the dominant spiritual symbols of our unity, acting, as they did, as mirrors reflecting our humanity, enabling us to see the "family " diaspora newly whole. We were many more in number, more varied, more sophisticated, but still "family." The "common good," though challenged more frequently with self-aggrandizing temptations, escapist distraction, and the heightened stress of dealing daily with inequities, remained paramount for the overwhelming majority. I was no longer just listening to stories about the kind of living that celebrates the interdependence of the individual and her community, now I was beginning to live my generation's contribution to the saga. Harlem was my home through mid-adolescence. I returned as an adult to teach in its public schools.

Wholeness is important to me, a wholeness comprised of distinct parts. The spirit of life running through each human being binds us, each to the other, making each of us whole, and making all of us together a whole. I believe that it is this interconnectedness of all life that is the symbol of the Divine. As a Unitarian Universalist I recognize the First and Seventh Principles of our Guiding Principles as a fitting frame for all seven of our Guiding Principles. The First Principle affirms "the inherent worth and dignity of every person," the Seventh Principle affirms "respect for the interdependent web of all existence of which we are a part." Within each of the seven principles there is an implicit call to action to create justice where justice is lacking, to gather-in all humankind leaving no one behind, to nurture and support the members of our human family, to reject facile answers that belie complex truths. A traditional emphasis on deed over creed reflects Unitarian Universalist belief that the spiritual life must be expressed in ethical behavior. Unitarian Universalist minister David Rhys Williams has stated, "We are joined together by a mystic oneness whose source we may never know, but whose reality we can never doubt. We are our neighbor's keeper, because that neighbor is but our larger self."

With the killing of Amadou Diallo* I keenly felt the rupture in our national family. As an African American human being part of me dies with Amadou, and as that same African American human being I grieve over the wound our family of humankind endures. I mourn and protest that we—all of us—have allowed this to happen again. We live such separate lives, for the most, with different sets of experiences in the public world, based on race. If you are not a person of color you can be completely unaware that experiences based on color are common occur-

---

*Amadou Diallo was an unarmed African immigrant who was shot by four New York City policemen, Kenneth Boss, Sean Carroll, Edward McMellon, and Richard Murphy on February 4, 1999. They fired nineteen bullets into Diallo as he was entering his Bronx apartment. The officers were later acquitted of murder.

rences. It is only when a tragedy of the magnitude of the Diallo killing, or the brutalization of Abner Louima,** or the killing of Anthony Baez*** occurs that patterns of police abuse are revealed; or when, longstanding complaints of police abuse of power against African American and Hispanic drivers are finally investigated in public hearings.

We know so little of our racial history together. Black history and white history are taught separately as if they were not taking place in the same country. The documentary "Africans in America," shown on television last fall, startled our intellect with details of our common history. We Africans and Europeans struggled over the meaning of freedom shaping our country in ways that would affect us for centuries. Why is it we don't know more about black and white cooperation where it existed: black and white abolitionists working together; white Underground Railroad "stations" that hid African Americans as they escaped north to Canada? Many questions are being asked currently of ourselves and others; let us not avoid the difficult ones. What kind of society are we willing to accept? Is a color-coded two standard policy of policing necessary to keep crime down? How much do we let others speak for us in the crucial area of race relations? Do we allow structures not of our making to make decisions for us?

Some of us will put our questions on the agenda of our church, or synagogue, or mosque. Particularly the question that asks: How can we repair the break in our sacred connection to one another?

**Abner Louima was sodomized and tortured by a New York City policeman, Justin Volpe, when Volpe mistakenly believed Louima had punched him as police tried to quell a disturbance on August 9, 1997. The officer, Volpe, pleaded guilty to charges of assault and was convicted on assault charges.
***Anthony Baez was choked to death during an encounter with police officer Francis Livoti on December 22, 1994. Livoti was acquitted of murder in 1996 but was subsequently fired from the New York City Police Force.

Questions for Writing and Discussion

1. What does Stawsky mean by "the interdependent web"? How is her point of view different from Hurston's?
2. Write a response to Stawsky, responding to the ideas in her letter. Write a letter of your own in which you connect with what she is

saying about race and identity. Make some suggestions on your own as to how her concerns could be addressed.

Mark Mathabane's *From the Far Side*

So far we have discussed those whose ancestors were enslaved and brought here. Since the United States is still perceived to be racist and elitist as a society, how do recent African immigrants fare in our society?

Mark Mathabane came to the United States in 1979 from South Africa. He thought he would be coming to the promised land. He was anxious to escape from a closed society and enter a more open one. The following is an essay he wrote that appears in *Race: How Blacks and Whites Feel about the American Obsession* (Terkel 1992).

My understanding of black life in America was largely based on reading *Ebony* and *Essence*. And my encounters with black superstar athletes and entertainers. These men and women had wealth and power and seemingly had independence from whites. So I concluded that racism had been abolished in America. The sacrifices made by Dr. King, Malcolm X, and all the unsung heroes and heroines had not been in vain. Equality and racial harmony had been achieved.

I saw all these people in the movies. It was back in those days when they were invited to South Africa to perform before integrated audiences, so the government could use their visits to publicize the lie that apartheid had ended.

My Uncle Pietrus loved those magazines. In every way, he copied the trends in America. He straightened his hair with those creams to make it less kinky. He bleached his face to make lighter. He dressed very much like the glamorous blacks in the movies and advertisements. The thing he failed to copy was their accent. This was a source of great frustration to him. If he could manage that, the masquerade would be complete. He could then qualify for the status of honorary white.

Racial classification was instilled in black people: the idea that you could escape the indignities and oppression if you became white. Many of those called "colored" have spent all their lives trying to pass for whites. There was a time when tests were conducted to determine if you belonged to one race or the other. In one, they ran a pencil through your hair, and if the pencil got entangled, you were summarily classified as black. If you had been white until then, you were promptly declassified as black. Families were torn apart.

Uncle Cheeks was the more militant because his life had been spent in jails. He was often arrested for general crimes. When he was denied a way to earn a living, he turned to robbery. He robbed the suburbs. When he came out of prison, he was a bitter man. But he was also possessed of a certain wisdom. I remember after I had shocked the family around the campfire reading the Declaration of Independence, about men being equal in the pursuit of happiness, he said, "Let me give you a little wisdom, for what it's worth."

He said, "Nephew, I may not know America, but I know the white man. Wherever blacks and whites have been together, and whites had the power, the blacks must be their slaves." I countered, "Uncle, what do you say about Arthur Ashe, Sidney Poitier, and Belafonte?" He said, "I still insist. Racism may exist in America."

My first encounter with America led me to conclude there was something terribly wrong. When I arrived in Gaffney, South Carolina, to start at Limestone College, I discovered this town was constituted of two worlds. The whites lived in relative opulence. They had paved streets, clean and decent homes. The black world was steeped in poverty, pain, and suffering. It was the very same poverty, pain, and suffering that I had left in Alexandria and Soweto.

I hadn't been familiar with the North. In fact, I couldn't distinguish between different parts of the United States. I had an offer to go to Princeton but I took the one to Limestone simply because I couldn't tell the difference. I began to hear and read that Freedom Fighters from the North, men and women, black and white, came down to the South to end this oppression and that there was much pain and bloodshed and death involved. Life was said to be better in the North. So I began to move from college to college, eventually ending up at a small one in the North, Dowling College on Long Island.

Many black students, as well as whites, were oblivious to the heroic struggles fought for the mothers and fathers and grandparents to win them the right to vote and to attend decent schools. That shocked me because if you forget that crucial part of your history, where can you get the resolve to protect what has been won by blood and sweat and toil?

When I told them about apartheid, they failed to see the connection to their own struggle here. Racism in America tended to be seamless, yet it was pervasive. They showed the same indifference and apathy of their white counterparts. The irony is that many came from poor families and were on financial aid.

For six, seven years, I was leading a schizophrenic life up North. Not to know what you're fighting against, to be constantly banging your head against invisible walls, it kills your soul. There were times when I longed for the world of apartheid. People would say, "How can you long for that abominable world?" At least in South Africa, I knew what I was fighting against. I knew what the limits were, so I could brace myself. Here I am told I'm free, I'm the equal of everyone, fair play is the name of the game. Yet, try as many of us do we seem to get nowhere.

I spent so much time, so much heartache in search of an apartment in New York. I would call on the phone and they would say, "Oh, we have a lovely front ocean home for you to see." They were deceived by my accent. They thought I was British. When I appeared a few hours later, well-dressed, suit, tie, and all, I'd be told the place was rented. I didn't drink, I didn't smoke, I did nothing to lead them not to rent me the room. It had taken two hours to reach this place, by train, ferry, and subway. I had a white friend call and he was told the apartment was still available. To me, who had lived in South Africa under the Group Areas Act, there was no difference, really.

So I decided to go back to the South, where you know where you stand. I would at least know who my true friends are. And my enemies. I was surprised to find that because of the civil-rights struggle, the few changes that have taken place toward integration have been more genuine and have had admirable results.

At my first attempt, I was shown a dozen apartments. All had white managers eager to show me the best. This was in Greensboro, North Carolina, where the first sit-ins occurred. It was cosmopolitan, integrated; I never experienced a rebuff.

There were people who didn't like me. The Ku Klux Klan marched, but I knew it as the Klan. I also knew when I gained acceptance, it was genuine. The discovery I made was that virulent racism had been transferred to northern cities, places like Howard Beach, Yonkers, Chicago, Boston. They were torn apart, polarized by emotions which not too long ago were thought to be the exclusive preserve of the South.

I asked myself: Why? The answers I came up with: Despite slavery and Jim Crow, the black and white people lived in close proximity and knew each other. Whereas in the North, before the black migrations, their acceptance was intellectual and theoretical. When they began to move into the cities, into the workplace, into the schools, into the neighborhoods, they had to be dealt with as a real presence. The reaction was a visceral one, full of hate.

When people heard me speak, they suddenly judged me differently. One time I said, "I know American blacks who speak English well. Why are they regarded different from me?" They went into convoluted explanations: "No, we're not prejudiced at all." What I discovered was that I didn't approach them with the hostility and anger that they perceived black Americans had. I could see a little bit of truth in that. I had gone beyond my anger and hate because of my South African experiences. When I approached a white person, I gave him the benefit of the doubt. There was little confrontation. It's doubly difficult for black Americans to avoid being angry or tense, because they've been through the furnace of racism and have been burned.

The reality is a mixed bag. It depends largely on who you meet first. If you meet a black mugger, your experience will be different from encountering a reasonable, sensitive, and proud black person. Very few whites have ever set foot in Harlem. In South Africa, there's a law that forbids whites from entering a ghetto. In America, there is no such law in effect. So what's to prevent you from using the stereotypes you see on television every night: murder, mugging, crime? It's very easy to say, "I don't go there because look who they are."

There is a legitimate fear, of course. It arises from the fact that black communities are disintegrating. The family structure has almost been decimated. In South Africa, we were deprived of much of everything through apartheid. But the one thing we refused to let go was our sense of family. It's the one thing that endures. There were midnight raids on the home of my parents for the crime of living together as husband and wife. Yet they stayed together because they knew how important it was psychologically to us children growing up.

I have seen it happen here, with the husband forbidden to be in the house of a welfare mother. I oppose that with every fiber of my being because I know how important a stable family structure is.

The city is oftentimes inhuman. The bond that ties people together is shattered by much of city life. I remember the feeling of community, where, as a child, if I go wrong and my parents are away, the neighbor will look after me, where we go next door for sugar or a piece of bread and get it. That seldom happens today in the city. The spirit of community still lives in small hamlets. That's why I live in Kernersville.

My wife and I had problems with black and white people. Some blacks wondered how I could contemplate marrying a white person when I'd been through the oppression of apartheid. They felt I had to be more angry toward white people. I knew from childhood that anger and hatred can be blinding and lead toward self-destruction. I almost died at one time because those passions were consuming me. I was about fourteen or fifteen and right in the thick of the schoolchildren's marches through Soweto. We had to fight for our rights because our parents were so battle-weary. I was saved because my mother told me, "You must learn to look at people's hearts." She did.

White individuals were the ones who kept me from being consumed by the anger I felt because of such injustice. I knew I should resist condemning white people as a group to perdition because the police mowed us down.

The reason I was able to go to school was because a white nun helped me get that paper without which I could not register. The only way I was able to learn to read and write, to break the shackles in my mind, was because a white family gave me those books which were denied in tribal schools. The only way I was able to come to America was because a white American tennis pro, Stan Smith, gave me an opportunity which my country had denied me. How can I deny my senses that there are white people who are different? I couldn't live with myself. A sweeping judgment is very dangerous.

It was painful for me when I was told marrying a white woman was a betrayal of the race, that it was a sign of disrespect for the black woman. I answered: "On the one hand you say segregation is wrong, the Mixed Marriages Act is wrong, the Group Areas Act has to go. I agree with you, because individuals have to be free to do as they please as long as they don't harm others. If you say that is wrong, how can you say a black person cannot befriend or marry a white person in the name of black pride? How can you justify that which you abominate in white people?"

My family was fully and openly and lovingly accepting of my wife. She herself comes from a family with a strong liberal tradition. Her father, a minister, was chased from his church and run out of town in Texas because he rented his house to a black family.

Nevertheless, there are liberals in the name only, who support integration—but when it comes *home,* they have a different feeling. My wife stood her ground. Sometimes people focus too much on what I had to go through, but they don't understand what she had to overcome.

Most of the trouble is with the male, black and white. We know that in slavery days the white male violated the black woman with impunity. Among some black men, having sexual relations with a white woman is seen as a conquest. I find this painful because you're dealing with human feelings, and people get hurt. It's treating the relationship of man and woman in a cynical, power-driven way. It's no different from what a white male does. You have acquired the same bestiality he had when your women were his slaves. You have confirmed what he always wanted you to be.

The reasonable black man ought to be wary of playing that power game. In the end, it compromises something very important, something black people have cherished a long time ago. It is despite how they are treated by white people, they will resist fighting back in kind. If we suffer from racism, by fighting back in a racist way, we confirm the prejudice of those who began it.

Oftentimes, the problems that afflict the poor and the powerless are not racial. They're problems between the haves and the have-nots. I have met poor whites. I befriended one who walked to school wearing his sister's panties because his family couldn't afford to buy him underwear. They used a propped-up door as a table. They were exploited by the gentry not because they were black. They were as white as the people who oppressed them.

South Africa is a mirror in which I see a lot of America. There are black yuppies who are very conservative. They work for multinational companies and drive BMW's. They act as a buffer between the privileged few and the aspirations of the many. They say, "Yes, apartheid is wrong, but you don't need to radically change the society." The only thing that distinguishes the two societies is that here there is a rule of law and of institutions that act as checks and balances. These are under siege today because politicians without backbone are abandoning causes to the prevailing wind of public opinion.

Today many people believe there is no longer any need for civil rights. Many believe there is no longer any need for unions. There is no longer any need for holding authority accountable. Reagan was never held accountable for any of the things he did. To blindly follow custom is the danger that faces America.

Tomorrow looks a bit sad because of the nature of the current generation. The older ones have been conservative and their contemporaries who fought them are battle-weary. In the past, the visionary force was in the young. But if the young are more conservative than their elders, we're in for it. Perhaps there will be a change in the nineties. Something seems to be in the wind. I hope.

America, as I learned as a South African high-school boy, was born out of struggle. The Revolution in this country was inspired by the Enlightenment. Yet liberalism today has become a dirty word. Yet what gave birth to our finest hours in America? The American Revolution was not a conservative one. It was a liberal, radical revolution.

Questions for Writing and Discussion

1. How does Mathabane compare the North and South with regard to the attitudes he found toward racism?
2. What does the author mean by "invisible walls"?
3. Why did he prefer to return to the South to look for a place to live?
4. How did he feel that people judged him differently when they heard him speak with his British-sounding accent? Why do you think this difference existed?
5. What fears does Mathabane have for the African American community here?
6. What problem did he and his wife encounter as a couple with both whites and blacks?
7. In what ways does the American society resemble that of South Africa?

Racism: Where Are We Today?

Between the time Zora Neale Hurston wrote and when Mark Mathabane and May Stawsky wrote, there may have been changes in American Society. The 1950s saw the beginning of the civil rights movement, while the 1960s brought the ethnic pride and "Black Is Beautiful" movements. The symbolic but significant evolution of nomenclature for those of African heritage, from Negroes to Blacks to African Americans, has been accompanied by solid examples of growth: the emergence of African American leaders in most parts of society; the integration of American institutions of all kinds; the passage of civil rights legislation; and the emergence of the black middle class.

However, the 1960s have long passed, and with increasing socioeco-nomic stratification, racism is still alive. In June 2000 the *New York Times* featured an editorial titled "Race in America" (*New York Times* 2000), in which it announced a journalistic investigation carried out over the previous year into race relations in the United States, an effort to build on President Clinton's 1997 call for national "conversations" about race. The articles resulting from the investigative reporting on race and race relations were published over a six-week period and revealed the continuing struggles we face as a nation to achieve true equality and integration. For example, one article examined what happened when African Americans joined an all-white Pentecostal church in Atlanta; it described their struggle to coexist and the pastor's role in the church's existence. Another reported on the state of race relations in the Army. The editors reported that in nearly all cases, African Americans were more willing than whites to talk about race. Very few people, with the exception of those in the articles, were willing to talk about private attitudes about race. Yet, these very attitudes determine how well we will succeed as a multicolored nation in getting along with one another.

Indeed, according to Steinhorn and Diggs-Brown, a white and black pair of authors who researched this area, though the public culture of today's society in the United States is decidedly antiracist, private life is another matter. The results of a 1993 survey of white people in Minneapolis are telling: although two-thirds favored sending white children to a predominantly black school, only 7 percent said that they would send their own child. For the majority of people in our country, we remain integrated only in name, not in deed (Steinhorn and Diggs-Brown 1999, 12).

Furthermore, to the darker-skinned people of the Caribbean, Latin America, the Middle East, and India, this kind of discrimination often comes as a shock, because in their native countries the perception of skin color is quite different. In Mexico, darker skin is not a target of prejudice because of the historical background of the mixing of races by intermarriage. In *Hunger of Memory*, Rodriguez's mother, influenced by the skin-color prejudices here, tells her son to keep himself out of the sun in order to prevent his skin, already dark, from getting even darker (Rodriguez 1983, 119). Had the family lived in Mexico instead of California, a mestizo (mixed) nation with a variety of skin colors, her attitude likely would have been quite different.

Considering all the evidence that shows that racial conflict is still present in our society, educators and teachers must be sensitive to all issues on the topic of race including "white privilege" (the advantage Anglo white people have over black that is often unaware). We must provide a classroom environment in which all students of all colors feel safe and accepted.

Optional Activity: Video Viewing on the Topic of Race and Slavery

1. Rent one of these videos: *The Tuskegee Airmen, Glory, Beloved,* or *Amistad.* Watch it and write a one-page summary of the plot; then turn the page over and write a response. What did you find particularly moving or interesting? What did you learn about race relations?

2. According to an article in the *New York Times* by Margo Jefferson (June 10, 1999, sec. E, pp. 1–2), movies that focus in a serious way on racial issues rarely do well at the box office. Do you think that this is merely a reflection of the American public's preference for escapist entertainment, or might the reason be more complicated? Explain.

Chapter 8

The American Identity and Education

What Is an American Identity?

We have read excerpts from six authors whose writing is testament to the ability to communicate in a second language. Their writings are meditations on identity and the self, on what it means to be exiled from one's native land and the resultant split in one's perception that can result in romantic nostalgia for the lost home. In many ways we are all exiles, looking for a new place to be at home. Whether one moves across town, country, or ocean, there are a compromised self and a sense of loss and the related coping strategies; at the same time, there is also a gathering of expectations, of renewal. With a new home comes a set of opportunities to reinvent oneself, even to live one's dream.

While language is only part of the acculturation and adjustment process, it is a central part. The writers we have read and discussed will tell you, perhaps, that not only is their new hyphenated self present in English but often that the old linguistic vestiges are present too—at the most a nuance here or an unusual word or expression there. All the authors from Rodriguez to Tan express a perception that results from having lived in more than one social and cultural context. In their words, there is a different sensibility in which all the selves are felt—past, present, and future, reflecting a complex awareness, a result of having lived in more than one context (Bakhtin 1996).

As educators, what identity are we asking students to assume in the context of socialization? The historical vision of a land of prosperity—where gold would be available to those who came to a new place—is far from the reality today for immigrants who come to the United States. The American Dream is still available to the rich and privileged, but opportunity can be difficult to obtain for those who are from ethnic, linguistic, or racial minorities. Poverty further complicates the situation of many; though we are publicly behind the democratic principle of the dignity of each human being, in actual fact, the United States is more of a class society than we often realize.

In order to obtain opportunity, the newly arrived individual learns that he or she has to adopt what would be considered the American middle-class identity. Above all, the newly arrived individual is told to learn English. The problem with this demand is that the immigrant is confronted with many kinds of American identities. There are multiple identities, not just one stereotype.

Exactly what is the American identity? What do we mean when we ask people "to be an American"? To what standard do we want people to acculturate? Is it the one depicted in the media, most notably television and movies? If one heeds the media, what ideas are being conveyed? Think about it. As a culture, are we promulgating the idea that we are all anorexically thin, violent, affluent, and sexually active? Are these the traits we want the newly arrived to assume? Are we trying to teach the values of competition, conquest, exploitation, and fragmentation of families for the sake of wealth? Is it no wonder that we are seeing violence increase in our schools? The episodes in Littleton, Colorado, and Jonesboro, Arkansas, reflect these "characteristics."

Examples abound in the movies and in literature. The movie *Grand Canyon* (1991) depicts a society torn apart by greed, power, and class-struggle racism. Like the lead character in Arthur Miller's *Death of a Salesman* and Nick in F. Scott Fitzgerald's novel *The Great Gatsby*, the individual is often disappointed in the reward brought by overemphasis on materialism: emotional bankruptcy and spiritual emptiness (Campbell and Alasdair 1997). Can you think of other examples in literature and film?

When they immigrate, the authors who live lives in two languages encounter an American culture in search of an identity. Now, in a new millennium, we are still a people in search of a national self. Yet the multiple possibilities and multiple identities are fascinating to writers such as the ones whose work is excerpted in this text, the "hybrid Americans" inhabiting the "borderlands of identity," skipping to and fro between identities and languages (Anzaldua 1987). Searching for the ideal wholeness and integrity of self, many immigrants fall short of their goal and settle into a permanently fragmented identity and have to learn to be content living compartmentalized existences. They learn to manipulate multiple identities politically, socially, and economically. For example, an individual could rely on her minority status to get into a college, rely on her American identity on the job where English is mandatory, and rely on still another ethnic identity to make and maintain social ties and friendships. A more integrated response can exist where an individual, while focusing on one main identity, admits to having others rather than keeping aspects of the self separate and hidden one from the other. This would be illustrated by an immigrant claiming only to be "American" while keeping his or her indigenous identity a secret.

For those of us who are in the field of education, our experience shapes how we teach language or any other subject. Every pedagogy is a value-based pedagogy to an extent, even if, at the same time, there are pedagogical, theoretical bases for what is taught (Freeman and Richards 1996). Our perspectives on any topic will determine not only what is taught but what is not taught and how it is to be done. Anyone involved in education needs to take stock of how comfortable he or she is with identity, in order to teach toward the goal of an integrated personality, one in which all the aspects of identity are at home with one another. As educators, we need to be at home in our own culture and comfortable with our own set of values in order to accept students from other cultures. We can learn much about adaptation and cognitive flexibility from bilingual students.

Becoming at home with oneself is a lifetime goal; it does not belong only to immigrants from other countries. A writer I know, an academic whom we will call Lila, is planning a move to California from the East Coast, a move of economic necessity. She reports the same "anomie" that the writers and characters in the movies we have been studying in this text felt. She feels the same sense of shakiness in her public and private self that Rodriguez described. Her story is similar to that of many immigrants; she was born in the deep South and felt she had to reinvent herself in order to feel as if she fit in as a citizen of New York. She hid her identity for a long time, feeling that northerners looked down on southerners. Lila learned to speak in the northeastern American English accent and to dress in dark colors, even in summer. Lila says she still brings out her southern accent when she returns home; this is her "private language." This change in sound still startles her family and others who have grown used to her acquired northern speech.

In order to cope, Lila, like Eva Hoffman, triangulates between the past in the East, the future in the West, and the present transitional identity. Lila also reports a certain feeling of detachment, what Czech author Milan Kundera (1984) called a "lightness of being." She knows that this move means she must completely reinvent herself, reestablish herself, find a new job, find a place to live, make new friends, create a whole new life, and become part of a new context.

To a lesser extent, she will experience anomie at first. Like the Chicana writer Gloria Anzaldua and the Vietnamese-African-French writer T. Minh-ha Trinh (1989), she hopes to invent a new identity with her hybrid southern-eastern-western experience. She will learn to switch off and on her southern dialect, among other things. She will observe her new surroundings, like an anthropologist, and slowly will "acculturate" herself to the new place and "culture."

Question for Writing and Discussion

Have you ever had an experience like Lila's?

Reasons Why Successful Immigrants Succeed

What is it that makes it easier for some individuals to accomplish the transition to a new place and to adjust successfully to a new life? Will Lila's strategies be successful? Think about the resources that may help an individual in this type of situation. What helped the writers whose work appears in this book?

Personal Resources

Like Chang-rae Lee, Lila has a work identity as professor and writer. She can transfer these skills to the new context. In Nieto's research (1996), the immigrant students who were successful had a talent or identity other than their native and public ones that helped them establish themselves in another domain, outside of their public and private lives. For students who are intellectually exceptional, and precociously intelligent, like some of the daughters in *Joy Luck Club*, the personal resources and talents will translate just fine into the new culture. But what about those who aren't so lucky?

Strong Family Ties

Immigrants who have strong family ties are likely to benefit and prevail, while those whose families are fragmented or dysfunctional may be at a disadvantage. Even where there is divorce or separation in the family, if the child has a strong relationship with a family member who could act as a mentor or role model, acculturation will be helped considerably. Family ties strengthen the private identity and language, and this strength can be transferred to the emerging identity. Though her aunts and siblings were in the Dominican Republic while she was in the United States, Julia Alvarez benefited from being part of a loving extended family with whom she was always in communication. The fact that her three sisters were experiencing the same things she was helped her too.

Language Identity

There is no question that the development of public and private identities is important. There can be other identities as well. Case study research by Zentella (1997) and others has suggested that the more comfortable a student is speaking and communicating in both native and second languages, the better able he or she will be to learn in both. Furthermore, those whose sense of self permits moving back and forth from language to language without suffering loss of identity are more likely to succeed academically, socially, and professionally (Martin 1999). Denying the native language and culture can be debilitating. In these situations, one must be open to owning all selves and the possibilities and opportunities afforded. As we saw, Richard Rodriguez suffered from the loss of his native language and the emotional support that was lost with it.

Spiritual or Religious Values

In Nieto's case study research (1996), Avi spoke of his religion and the discipline and personal integrity that his beliefs and his membership in his Jewish culture brought to him (Nieto, 117). Eva Hoffman spoke of her mother's teaching her to be proud of her Jewish identity (Hoffman, 144). In a changing world with shifting values, spiritual teachings of the world's religions can help people develop boundaries and strong self-esteem.

Personal Characteristics

Some people are, by their nature, more open to change. These individuals will find a new context, language, and culture challenging rather than intimidating. In his book *A Fine Line*, Eviatar Zerubavel (1991) discusses how a rigid mind abhors change (115). The rigid mind has set boundaries, where definitions are fixed. A flexible mind, while recognizing that boundaries are necessary for organization and order, also admits that this organization can be restructured and changed with the human potential for growth. There is a "happy medium" between extreme rigidity and extreme fluidity that allows for restructuring as the human potential for growth and change allows us to reenvision our way of classifying human experience (Zerubavel 1991, 122).

Individuals who allow for perceptual flexibility seem to be more open to change, to avoid stereotyping as a shortcut for thinking, and constantly and creatively evolve as they experience life. These individuals do not need to give away all structure to do this. They tend to evaluate each situation and each individual as unique and worthy of respect. They are open to learning about new cultures, new languages, and new ways of being. They avoid shortcuts, like racial, gender-based, or ethnic stereotyping. Their boundaries appear to be made of rubber, not cement. This kind of thinking requires a strength of character, a willingness to "be different" if necessary, knowing that it will be beneficial to themselves and society in the long run. For example, Zora Neale Hurston demonstrated a flexibility and versatility in her life and career, as did Eva Hoffman.

Lila has many personal characteristics that will help her in her new life in the West. A loyal person, she has strong family ties in the South and in the East that support her move to California. She is deeply spiritual, an Episcopalian, and has made contact with a church in the town in California where she will be living with her husband. She has mastered the "Yankee" dialect and speaks Spanish fluently. A dedicated teacher who loves to connect with students, she hopes that her ability in Spanish together with her graduate degrees and experience in education will help her land a job in ESL or linguistics. She has other abilities, as well. Like Eva Hoffman, she is a pianist and hopes to find a chamber group in which she can play classical music. Through her new job, her church, or her music hobby, she most likely will meet many people and make friends, making her adjustment to her new milieu easier.

Mostly, however, her ability to adjust will stem from her willingness to develop a flexible, multicultural outlook, integrating her Southern and Eastern self with the Western one. Her attitude tends to be positive, rather than negative, neither idealizing nor romanticizing the West, but looking forward to living through another adventure and learning new ways of thinking, seeing, and existing. As Mary Catherine Bateson put it in *Peripheral Visions: Learning Along the Way* (1994), she is able to develop and maintain a point of view that takes into consideration cultures other than her own, whether the culture be western U.S. or Latino or Chinese.

She knows, like the authors whose works are excerpted in this book, that we are not to assume we know someone based on information we have heard or read about people from their group; we must avoid stereotyping. We must learn that each individual is unique and that many factors form a person's identity. Living with those from other cultures is a creative art; living with those from younger generations is like living with immigrants because the young individuals have been born into a different world that neither we nor our parents have experienced (Bateson 2000). We must learn to create an identity and compose a life that is open to other viewpoints, customs, languages, and traditions, yet finds commonality in that we are all part of a human culture (Bateson 1994). We all, no matter what our backgrounds, have human needs in common. However, there are many differences that enrich the human experience that we must acknowledge and interpret in a positive manner whenever possible.

Where there are destructive customs, if we are open to one another, we can benefit one another by sharing knowledge that can positively affect future generations. For example, there are still many cultures where women are not valued except in their roles as wives and mothers; they are not allowed to own property and are under the jurisdiction of the males in the community, not even allowed to leave home (Mernissi 1994). These women can, if they are open to customs from other cultures where men and women are treated more equally, imagine and perhaps someday live in a more egalitarian culture. At the very least, they can encourage and teach their children about the possibility of a more just society.

We must encourage children to develop a strong sense of self that enables them to feel free to learn new ways of seeing and learning. Multiculturalism must be included in our sense of self at a deeper level; it is more than a token concept that can divide and build animosity between vying groups. By understanding one's own roots and background, one becomes more sensitive to another's. If we can become comfortable with who we are, then we can be more accepting of others.

Positive Role Models

Both young boys and girls need strong, positive role models with whom they can identify. This is especially important when the family is split up or when parents as role models are missing or dysfunctional. Chang-rae Lee's novel *Native Speaker* is largely focused on men who in many ways were father figures to Henry Park, from the time he was a child and on into his adult and professional life. Gilligan recommends that there be more women who can be role models for adolescent girls (Gilligan and Brown 1994).

Dispelling the Myths

As educators, we must know that when we teach, we teach values such as self-discipline and compassion. We have a responsibility to dispel myths about minority and immigrant students. What we believe informs our pedagogy. Let's examine some of the more common myths associated with minority and immigrant students.

Myth 1: *They know language well if they can speak it with reasonably good pronunciation.*
Truth: Many immigrants know a few words, and some can pronounce some words exceptionally well. That does not mean that they know how to read and write fluently or have a good vocabulary in the second language. Learning a new language is a complicated process.

Myth 2: *They came here of their own free will.*
Truth: Children are rarely part of the decision-making process that brought them to a new country, and sometimes this also is true of adults (those who are seeking asylum, for example).

Myth 3: *They are undermotivated if they do not speak English well.*
Truth: Most people want to speak English shortly after they arrive here. For some, timidity is a problem, or a number of other emotional/social situations. Also, learning to communicate well in a new language is not something that happens overnight.

Myth 4: *They do not suffer from discrimination based on their ethnicity.*
Truth: If individuals have different skin color or other physical characteristics, they are likely to have some difficulty and will be made to feel self-conscious. Unfortunately, the United States isn't a color-blind country.

Myth 5: *They have forgotten all they learned in school in their native land.*
Truth: Not only will they not have forgotten, they will be experiencing a whole new kind of schooling, in all likelihood. Classrooms in most other countries are usually more teacher-centered, for one thing. Expect that your students will need a lot of explanation and models as to how to "do" school here.

Myth 6: *They don't want to be thought of as American.*

Truth: Most immigrants are proud to be thought of as American with a hyphenated identity, for example, "Mexican-American," and so on. They have a great respect for this country and its democratic ideals. But, they also want to retain the pride they have in their native language and culture.

Myth 7: *The parents do not come to the school or help with their children's homework because they don't care.*

Truth: This is complicated. Most often, the parents are working and likely not, at least initially, in 9–5 jobs, which makes it difficult to come to school. Many also do not understand English or are self-conscious about how they speak. Some are overwhelmed with other aspects of parenting. They also may not realize how the American educational system emphasizes parental involvement.

Myth 8: *Class distinction in their native countries doesn't matter to most immigrants. Once they have arrived here, they are all in the same class. This is the United States, an egalitarian country.*

Truth: There are different classes in all cultures. In some cultures, there are more extreme differences in class. Therefore, just because two people are from the same country doesn't mean they will identify with one another. They may be from different societal classes. India is an example of a democracy that has a class system.

Final Activity

1. Interview a student who is taking English as a second language course.
2. Write a summary of the interview.
3. Analyze the story the interview tells. How does it reflect what we have discussed in this chapter?
4. Does your interviewee reflect what you have also learned from any of the writers excerpted in this textbook? How? Why?
5. Can you give examples of other myths about immigrant students and cite ways to dispel them?
6. What tips would you pass on to Lila or anyone else you know who is facing a big change in their life?

7. If you were planning to go outside the United States to teach, how could you help prepare yourself psychologically and emotionally for living in a new country and experiencing a new culture?

In addtion to the authors whose work is excerpted in this book, the writers listed in Appendix 1 can further the exploration of identity and culture. A list of videos that depict cultural experience is included as Appendix 2.

Appendix 1
Recommended Readings

Alvarez, Julia. 1992. *How the Garcia Girls Lost Their Accents*. New York: Plume.

Bateson, Mary Catherine. 1989. *Composing a Life*. New York: Penguin Books.

Cahill, Thomas. 1999. *The Gifts of the Jews*. New York: Doubleday.

Carter, Forrest. 1986. *The Education of Little Tree*. Albuquerque: University of New Mexico Press.

Castillo-Speed, Lilian, ed. 1995. *Latin: Women's Voices from the Borderlands*. New York: Simon and Schuster.

Chang, Pang-Mei. 1996. *Bound Feet and Western Dress*. Bantam Doubleday.

Cisneros, Sandra. 1989. *The House on Mango Street*. New York: Vintage Books.

Danticat, Edwidge. 1994. *Breath, Eyes, Memory*. New York: Random House (Vintage Books).

Díaz, Junot. 1996. *Drown*. New York: Riverhead Books.

Divakaruni, Chitra. 1997. *The Mistress of Spices*. New York: Anchor Books.

Fishkin, Barbara. 1997. *Muddy Cup: A Dominican Family Comes of Age in a New America*. New York: Scribner.

Garcia, Christina. 1992. *Dreaming in Cuban*. New York: Ballantine Books.

Graves, L. 1999. *A Woman Unknown: Voices from a Spanish Life*. London: Virago Press.

Hernandez, Carmen. 1997. *Puerto Rican Voices in English: Interviews with Writers*. Westport, CT: Praeger Publishers.

Keller, Nora Okja. 1997. *Comfort Woman*. New York: Penguin Books.

Kingsolver, Barbara. 1993. *Homeland*. New York: HarperCollins.

Kingston, Maxine Hong. 1993. *Woman Warrior*. New York: Random House.

Lahiri, Jhumpa. 1999. *The Interpreter of Maladies*. Boston: Houghton Mifflin.

Lee, Chang-rae. 1999. *A Gesture Life*. New York: Riverhead Books.

Lee, Gus. 1994. *China Boy*. Penguin Books.

Lee, Richard Borshay. "Eating Christmas in the Kalahari." *Anthropology* 98/99 (1998): 27–30.

Liu, Eric. 1998. *The Accidental Asian*. New York: Random House.

López, Tiffany Ana, ed. 1993. *Growing Up Chicana/o*. New York: Avon Books.

Mar, M. E. 1999. *Paper Daughter: A Memoir*. New York: HarperCollins.

Mernissi, Fatima. 1994. *Dreams of Trespass*. Reading, MA: Perseus Press.

Mones, Nicole. 1998. *Lost in Translation*. New York: Random House.

Mora, Pat. 1997. *House of Houses*. Boston: Beacon Press.

Morales, Aurora Levins. 1996. "Child of the Americas." In *Literature: Reading and Responding to Fiction, Poetry, Drama, and the Essay*, ed. Joel Wingard (Reading, MA: Addison Wesley Educational), 261.

Morrison, Toni. 1994. *The Bluest Eye*. New York: Plume.

Mukherjee, Bharati. 1991. *Jasmine*. New York: Random House.

Mura, David. 1996. *Turning Japanese*. New York: Anchor Books.

Nabokov, Vladimir. 1966. *Speak, Memory.* New York: Putnam.

Norberg-Hodge, Helena. 1991. *Ancient Futures.* San Francisco: Sierra Club Publishers.

Rose, Mike. 1989. *Lives on the Boundary.* New York: Penguin Books.

Santiago, Esmeralda. 1993. *When I was Puerto Rican.* New York: Addison Wesley.

———. 1998. *Almost a Woman.* Reading, MA: Perseus Publishers.

Tan, Amy. 1991. *The Kitchen God's Wife.* New York: Ivy Books.

———. 1995. *The Hundred Secret Senses.* New York: Putnam.

Trice, Dawn Turner. 1996. *Only Twice I've Wished for Heaven.* New York: Doubleday.

Appendix 2
Recommended Videos

The following videos address themes and issues discussed in this book.

Amistad; dir. Steven Spielberg (1997)
Bhaji on the Beach; dir. Gurinder Chadha (1994, Britain)
Bossa Nova; dir. Bruno Barreto (1999, Brazil)
Buena Vista Social Club; dir. Wim Wenders (1999)
Cookie's Fortune; dir. Robert Altman (1999)
Cry the Beloved Country; dir. Darrell Roodt (1995, South Africa)
East Is East; dir. Damien O'Donnell (1999, Britain)
Eat Drink Man Woman; dir. Ang Lee (1994, Taiwan)
El Norte; dir. Gregory Nava (1983, Spain)
Fable of the Beautiful Pigeon Fancier; dir. Ray Guerra (1988, Spain)
Glory; dir. Edward Zwick (1989)
Green Card; dir. Peter Weir (1990)
Hombres Armados (Armed men); dir. John Sayles (1997)
The Joy Luck Club; dir. Wayne Wang (1993)
La Familia (The Family); dir. Ettore Scola (1987, Italy)
Lone Star; dir. John Sayles (1995)
Mi Familia (My family); dir. Gregory Nava (1994)
Mississippi Masala; dir. Mira Nair (1992)
Mi Vida Loca (My crazy life); dir. Allison Anders (1994)
Moscow on the Hudson; dir. Paul Mazursky (1984)
Old Gringo; dir. Luis Puenzo (1989)
Out of Africa; dir. Sydney Pollack (1985)
The Perez Family; dir. Mira Nair (1995)
Picture Bride; dir. Kayo Hatta (1994, Japan)
Place of Weeping; dir. Darrell Roodt (1986, South Africa)
Pushing Hands; dir. Ang Lee (1992)
Raise the Red Lantern; dir. Zhang Yimou (1991, China)
The Scent of Green Papaya; dir. Tran Anh Hung (1993, Vietnam)
The Secret of Roan Inish; dir. John Sayles (1994)
The Tuskegee Airmen; dir. Robert Markowitz (1995)
Wedding Banquet; dir. Ang Lee (1993, Taiwan)
What's Cooking? dir. Gurinda Chadha (2000)

Bibliography

Aciman, A., ed. 1999. *Letters of Transit: Reflections on Exile, Identity, Language, and Loss.* New York: New York Public Library.

Akhtar, S. 1995. A third individuation: Immigration, identity, and the psychoanalytic process. *Journal of the American Psychoanalytic Association* 43 (4): 1051–79.

Alvarez, J. 1998. *Something to Declare.* New York: Algonquin Books of Chapel Hill.

———. 1997. *How the Garcia Girls Lost Their Accents.* New York: Algonquin Books of Chapel Hill.

Amati-Mehler, J., S. Argentieri, and J. Canestri. 1993. *The Babel of the Unconscious: Mother Tongue and Foreign Languages in the Psychoanalytic Dimension,* trans. J. Whitelaw-Cucco. Madison, CT: International University Press.

Anzaldua, G. 1987. *Borderlands/La Frontera: The New Mestiza.* California: Aunt Lute Books.

Bakhtin, M. M. 1996. *Speech Genres and Other Late Essays.* Austin: University of Texas Press.

Bateson, M. C. 1994. *Peripheral Visions: Learning along the Way.* New York: HarperCollins.

———. 2000. *Full Circles, Overlapping Lives: Culture and Generation in Transition.* New York: Random House.

Belenky, M., L. Bond, and J. Weinstock. 1997. *A Tradition That Has No Name.* New York: Basic Books.

Belenky, M., B. Clinchy, N. Goldberger, and J. Tarule. 1996. *Women's Ways of Knowing: The Development of Self, Voice, and Mind.* 10th anniversary ed. New York: HarperCollins.

Bloom, H., ed. 1986. *Zora Neale Hurston.* New York: Chelsea Publishers.

Brent, L. 1973. *Incidents in the Life of a Slave Girl.* Florida: Harcourt.

Campbell, N., and K. Alasdair. 1997. *American Cultural Studies: An Introduction to American Culture.* London: Routledge Publishers.

Cazden, Cancino, E. J. Rosansky, and J. Schumann. 1975. *Second Language Acquisition Sequence in Children, Adolescents and Adults.* U.S. Department of Health, Education, and Welfare, National Institutional Education Office of Research Grants C, Grant NE-6-00-3-0014.

Damon, W. 1999. The moral development of children. *Scientific American,* August, 72–78.

Ebert, R. 1995. Review of "My Family," dir. Gregory Nava. http://www.suntimes.com/ebert/ebert_reviews/1995/05/977621.html

Fishman, J. 1977. *Sociolinguistics.* Rowley, MA: Newbury House Publishers.

Freeman, D., and J. Richards. 1993. Conceptions of teaching and the education of second language teachers. *TESOL Quarterly* 27 (2): 203.

———. 1996. *Teaching Learning in Language Teaching.* New York: Cambridge University Press.

Garza-Guerrero, A. C. 1974. Culture shock: Its mourning and the vicissitudes of identity. *Journal of the American Psychoanalytic Association* 22:408–29.

Gates, H. L. 1993. *Zora Neale Hurston: Critical Perspectives Past and Present.* New York: Amistad Press.

Gee, J. 1992. *The Social Mind.* New York: Bergin and Garvey.

Genesee, F. 1994. *Educating Second Language Children.* New York: Cambridge University Press.

Gilligan, C., and L. Brown. 1992. *Meeting at the Crossroads.* New York: Ballantine Books.

Goffman, E. 1959. *The Presentation of Self in Everyday Life.* New York: Doubleday.

Goleman, D. 1995. *Emotional Intelligence.* New York: Bantam Books.

Graves, L. 1999. *A Woman Unknown: Voices from a Spanish Life.* London: Virago Press.

Gup, T. 1997. Who is a whiz kid? *Newsweek,* April 21, 21.

Harris-Hastick, E. 1996. Voices of Korean-American women. *Community Review,* City University of New York, 14:34.

Hemenway, R. 1977. *Zora Neale Hurston: A Literary Biography.* Urbana: University of Illinois Press.

Hoffman, E. 1989. *Lost in Translation: A Life in a New Language.* New York: Penguin Books.

———. 1993 *Exit into History.* New York: Viking Publishing.

———. 1998. *Shtetl: The Life and Death of a Small Town and the World of Polish Jews.* New York: Houghton Mifflin.

Hurston, Z. N. 1937. *Their Eyes Were Watching God.* New York: Harper and Row.

———. [1942] 1995. My people! My people! In *Dust Tracks on a Road.* New York: HarperCollins.

———. 1979. *I Love Myself When I Am Laughing and Again When I Am Looking Mean and Impressive,* ed. Alice Walker. New York: Feminist Press.

———. 1995. *The Complete Stories.* New York: HarperCollins.

Jefferson, M. 1999. Writing about race, walking on eggshells. *New York Times,* June 10, Sec. E, pp. 1–2.

Kostyal, K. M. 1995. Eternal Poland: Krakow and the Carpathians. *Traveler: National Geographic* 12 (2): 54–72.

Kundera, M. 1984. *The Book of Laughter and Forgetting.* New York: Penguin Books.

Lee, C. 1995. *Native Speaker.* New York: Penguin Books.

———. 1999. *A Gesture Life.* New York: Penguin Putnam.

Li, X. 1996. *Good Writing in Cross-cultural Context.* Albany: State University of New York Press.

Mar, M. E. 1999. *Paper Daughter: A Memoir.* New York: HarperCollins.

Martin, D. 1999. *Ethnic identity in second language learning.* Working paper. City Univeristy of New York Graduate Center.

Mathabane, M. 1992. From the far side. In *Race: How Blacks and Whites Feel about the American Obsession,* ed. S. Terkel. New York: Doubleday.

Mernissi, F. 1994. *Dreams of Trespass:Tales of a Harem Girlhood.* Reading, MA: Perseus Press.

Moghaddam, F., D. Taylor, and S. Wright. 1993. *Social Psychology in Cross-Cultural Perspective.* New York: Freeman and Company.

New York Times. 2000. Race in America. *New York Times,* 4 June. Sec. 4, p. 18.

Nieto, S. 1996. *Affirming Diversity.* White Plains, NY: Longman Publishers.

Nine-Curt, J. 1994. *Cross-Cultural Communication among Puerto Ricans and Anglos from a Non-Verbal Perspective.* Rio Piedras: University of Puerto Rico Press.

Roddenbury, G. 1995. In *Contemporary Authors,* vol. 110, ed. H. May, 429. Detroit: Gale Research.

Rodriguez, R. 1983. *Hunger of Memory: The Education of Richard Rodriguez.* New York: Bantam Books.

———. 1992. *Days of Obligation: An Argument with My Mexican Father.* New York: Viking Press.

Santana-Seda, O. S. 1975. A contrastive study in rhetoric: An analysis of the organization of English and Spanish paragraphs written by native speakers of each language. *Dissertation Abstracts International* 35 (10):6681A.

Schumann, J. 1978. Social and psychological factors in second language acquisition. In *Understanding Second and Foreign Language Learning,* ed. J. Richards, 163–78. Rowlen, MA: Newbury House Publishers.

Seelye, H. N. 1976. *Teaching Culture.* Skokie, IL: National Textbook Company.

Sennett, R., and J. Cobb. 1972. *The Hidden Injuries of Class.* New York: Norton Publishing.

Silber, N. 1993. *The Romance of Reunion: Northerners and the South.* Chapel Hill: University of North Carolina Press.

Steinhorn, L. and B. Diggs-Brown. 1999. *By The Color of Our Skin.* New York: Dutton.

Tan, A. 1989a. Two kinds. In *The Joy Luck Club.* New York: Ivy Books.

———. 1989b. Without wood. In *The Joy Luck Club.* New York: Ivy Books.

———. 1993. *The Kitchen God's Wife.* New York: Putnam Publishing.

———. 1995. *The Hundred Secret Senses.* New York: Putnam Publishing.

Tannen, D. 1990. *You Just Don't Understand: Women and Men in Conversation.* New York: Ballantine Books.

———. 1994. *Talking from 9 to 5: Women and Men in the Workplace: Language, Sex and Power.* New York: Avon Books.

Terkel, S. 1992. *Race: How Blacks and Whites Feel about the American Obsession.* New York: Doubleday.

Trinh, T. M. 1989. *Woman, Native, Other: Writing Postcoloniality and Feminism.* Bloomington: Indiana University Press.

Walker, A. 1975. In search of Zora Neale Hurston. *Ms. Magazine,* March, 74–79, 85–89.

Zentella, A. C. 1997. *Growing up Bilingual.* Malden, MA: Blackwell Publishers.

Zerubavel, E. 1991. *A Fine Line: Making Distinctions in Everyday Life.* Chicago: University of Chicago Press.